Lacan and Capitalist Discourse

Lacan and Capitalist Discourse explores the political and theoretical connections between the Covid-19 Pandemic and Capitalism, unravelling the direct consequences of Lacan's thesis of so-called "Capitalist Discourse,"

Jorge Alemán provides an account of neoliberalism, its mechanisms to produce subjectivities, and the new modes of the political far Right. The book begins with the problem of a possible exit from capitalism, continuing to consider the possibilities of mourning and the active production of a new Left. Jorge Alemán engages deeply with a range of thinkers: primarily Lacan, but also Heidegger, Marx, Laclau, Foucault, Butler, Badiou, Althusser, and others, in making his case.

Lacan and Capitalist Discourse will be of great interest to psychoanalysts and to academics of psychoanalytic and Lacanian studies, cultural theory, philosophy, and political thought.

Jorge Alemán is Doctor Honoris Causa of the Universidad Nacional de Rosario, Honorary Professor at the Universidad Nacional de Buenos Aires, the Universidad Nacional de San Martín, and the Universidad Nacional de Villa María Córdoba. He has published numerous essays on psychoanalysis, philosophy, and political thought.

Daniel Runnels is Assistant Professor of Spanish at the University of Central Missouri.

The Lines of the Symbolic in Psychoanalysis Series

Series Editor: Ian Parker
Manchester Psychoanalytic Matrix

Psychoanalytic clinical and theoretical work is always embedded in specific linguistic and cultural contexts and carries their traces, traces which this series attends to in its focus on multiple contradictory and antagonistic 'lines of the Symbolic'. This series takes its cue from Lacan's psychoanalytic work on three registers of human experience, the Symbolic, the Imaginary and the Real, and employs this distinctive understanding of cultural, communication and embodiment to link with other traditions of cultural, clinical and theoretical practice beyond the Lacanian symbolic universe. The Lines of the Symbolic in Psychoanalysis Series provides a reflexive reworking of theoretical and practical issues, translating psychoanalytic writing from different contexts, grounding that work in the specific histories and politics that provide the conditions of possibility for its descriptions and interventions to function. The series makes connections between different cultural and disciplinary sites in which psychoanalysis operates, questioning the idea that there could be one single correct reading and application of Lacan. Its authors trace their own path, their own line through the Symbolic, situating psychoanalysis in relation to debates which intersect with Lacanian work, explicating it, extending it and challenging it.

Speculating on the Edge of Psychoanalysis
Rings and Voids
Pablo Lerner

A Lacanian Conception of Populism
Society Does Not Exist
Timothy Appleton

On the History and Transmission of Lacanian Psychoanalysis
Speaking of Lacan
Chris Vanderwees

Lacan and Capitalist Discourse
Neoliberalism and Ideology
Jorge Alemán

For more information about the series, please visit: www.routledge.com/The-Lines-of-the-Symbolic-in-Psychoanalysis-Series/book-series/KARNLOS

Lacan and Capitalist Discourse

Neoliberalism and Ideology

Jorge Alemán

Translated from Spanish by Daniel Runnels

Routledge
Taylor & Francis Group

LONDON AND NEW YORK

First published in English 2024
by Routledge
4 Park Square, Milton Park, Abingdon, Oxon OX14 4RN

and by Routledge
605 Third Avenue, New York, NY 10158

Routledge is an imprint of the Taylor & Francis Group, an informa business

Originally published in Spain as:

Ideología by Jorge Alemán

© 2021, Ned Ediciones

All rights reserved by and controlled through Ned Ediciones

British Library Cataloguing-in-Publication Data
A catalogue record for this book is available from the British Library

ISBN: 978-1-032-52958-5 (hbk)
ISBN: 978-1-032-52957-8 (pbk)
ISBN: 978-1-003-40941-0 (ebk)

DOI: 10.4324/9781003409410

Typeset in Times New Roman
by Apex CoVantage, LLC

Contents

Acknowledgments

A special thanks to Daniel Runnels for his great work on this translation.

Given that I had the opportunity to sketch out some of the themes developed in this book in a Zoom seminar during Covid-19 confinement, I would like to thank all of those who formed a part of the organization of the "Ciclo de Conversaciones: La Época en Nosotrxs. Nosotrxs en la Época" ("Conversation Cycle: The Epoch in All of Us. All of Us in the Epoch"). What was gathered together in this cycle was wholly destined for the social dining halls of the Ministry of Community Development in the province of Buenos Aires. I would also like to name those who made this positive experience possible:

Axel Kicillof, Governor of the province of Buenos Aires; Andres Larroque, Minister of Community Development in the province of Buenos Aires; Nicolás Kreplak, Vice Minister of Health in the province of Buenos Aires; Julieta Calmels, Sub-Secretary of Mental Health, Problematic Consumption and Gender Violence in the province of Buenos Aires; Paula Biglieri, professor in the School of Philosophy and Letters at the University of Buenos Aires; Pablo Bilyk, Vice Dean of the School of Journalism and Social Communication at the National University of La Plata; Fabiana Rousseaux, Director of the Civil Association Clinical Territories of Memory.

During the seminar, I would like to highlight that both Pablo Bilyk and Fabiana Rousseaux coordinated the different conversations that, thanks to a serious and committed audience, were presented.

I would also like to give a special thanks to:

My friend Sergio Larriera for our topological conversations, conversations which gave rise to the figures and graphics that appear in the book.

My colleague Estela Canuto, who gave special attention to corrections of the text.

And finally, to my friend María Victoria Gimbel, whose expository clarity helped me to transform a mosaic of oral interventions, articles, and notes, into the present book.

Jorge Alemán

Series Preface for Jorge Alemán's *Lacan and Capitalist Discourse: Neoliberalism and Ideology*

Lacan briefly added a fifth 'discourse' to the 'four discourses' he had elaborated in his seventeenth seminar. That seminar had been designed to enable psychoanalysts to step back from their well-trod institutional practices and conceptualize where they were being placed in different forms of structured knowledge and subjectivity. The fifth discourse, the 'capitalist discourse,' is what Jorge Alemán now employs to analyze contemporary neoliberal capitalism. The four discourses – of the master, the university, the hysteric, and the analyst – operated as a series of formulas that each gave a distinct nuanced edge to what we understand by the master signifier, battery of signifiers, barred subject, and objet petit a.

The four discourses were susceptible, in the hands of many social theorists, to a kind of intuitive understanding – understanding that is part of the register of the Imaginary – and also appeared to give a satisfying Symbolic shape to the language that bears us. What we find in Lacan and now in Jorge Alemán in the addition of the fifth discourse is a dramatic mutation or twist in the movement of the discourses, something that also draws attention to what was always disruptive and unmanageable about capitalism, whether for those who pretended to master it or turn it into university knowledge, or those who rebelled against it or wanted to diagnose it.

The emergence of neoliberalism as the now globally-dominant form of capitalism at the moment shatters the old illusions about capitalism as part of the natural order of things and covers over this real with a new series of illusions – potent forms of ideology – that embed our subjectivity in a reality that is all the more entwined with power. Neoliberalism, remember, is not only the stripping away of the welfare functions of the capitalist state but also the intensification of individual responsibility so that those without any support are made to pay for the endemic crises that this political-economic system carries with it. Neoliberalism also entails the increasing securitization of everyday life, whether that is in the stepping up of police powers to deal with dissent or the intensely ideological punitive measures that are applied to those who are viewed as weak.

This book thus extracts a conceptual tool from Lacan's text and puts it to work, expanding the remit of psychoanalysis precisely because the cultural-political phenomena Lacan was pointing to have now become exorbitant, exaggerated, gross measures of the reality we inhabit. That requires a close reading and political re-reading of Lacan that also turns psychoanalysis into a form of treatment of the social conditions that produce the distress that we meet in the clinic; this book interprets the world in order to change it. Jorge Alemán, one of the foremost Lacanian political theorists in Argentina, thus also retrieves from Lacan, for us, a conceptualization of what it means to be an analyst that moves beyond diagnoses to intervention.

Psychoanalytic clinical and theoretical work circulates through multiple intersecting antagonistic symbolic universes. This series opens connections between different cultural sites in which Lacanian work has developed in distinctive ways, in forms of work that question the idea that there could be one single correct reading and application. The Lines of the Symbolic in Psychoanalysis series provides a reflexive reworking of psychoanalysis that transmits Lacanian writing from around the world, steering a course between the temptations of a metalanguage and imaginary reduction, between the claim to provide a god's eye view of psychoanalysis and the idea that psychoanalysis must everywhere be the same. And the elaboration of psychoanalysis in the symbolic here grounds its theory and practice in the history and politics of the work in a variety of interventions that touch the real.

Ian Parker
Manchester Psychoanalytic Matrix

Introduction

In this book, I aim to explain – theoretically and politically – some of the consequences that emerge between the pandemic and capitalism because, as is to be expected, much will change forever, and the effects will be felt in numerous spheres of life. These pages are filled with conjectures, readings, and intuitions coming from a community of voices. These "resonances" attempt to anticipate some possible paths derived from a sustained insistence that does not wish to cede and persists in a continual interrogation of the conditions of the emancipatory project.

In the different sections of this book, I use the Lacanian hypothesis of the capitalist discourse as one of the main levers that supports the exposition of ideas, open to different readings. The present book is presented in harmony with my two previous books – *Capitalismo. Crímen perfecto o emancipación* (*Capitalism. The Perfect Crime or Emancipation*) and *Pandemónium. Notas sobre el desastre* (*Pandemonium. Notes on the Disaster*), meaning that this book, despite being its own unit, can also be considered the third installment of a trilogy.

DOI: 10.4324/9781003409410-1

Chapter 1

Pandemic and Capitalism

To start, I suggest that one cannot analyze our era as if it were an "object" exterior to us because we are never contemporaneous with it. Here I aim to describe the different impacts to which the characterization of our era alludes in its internal relationship with the movement of capitalism. All this keeping in mind, as well, the effects that it brings into play regarding us, and even accepting the arbitrariness that the very term *us* carries with it. This word does not cancel the irreducible singularity of each one of us. Rather, it is about an *us* that never totalizes nor is reduced to unity, with there being problems that are difficult to articulate and that remain face-to-face with the opaque obstacle of their own dissatisfaction. As is often the case, I appeal here to what Lacan referred to as *capitalist discourse*, underlining once more its troubling circularity and its capacity for connecting places that used to be outside of industrial capitalism. The real of capitalist discourse is that it rejects impossibility by acting in such a way that everything appears possible to capture which might traverse the pandemic disaster.

The pandemic, which has intensified inequality to unknown limits in dominant Western countries, while not identical to the movement of capitalism, appears to be expanding with an analogous potentiality if we take into account the virality of Covid-19. On many occasions, I have marked the difference between the Lacanian capitalist discourse and master discourse, assigned to the period of Fordist industrial capitalism, where certain traditions and symbolic legacies had not yet disintegrated. Capitalist discourse primarily connects the subject to surplus enjoyment (*plus de jouir*), which allows us to consider the structure of neoliberalism in relation to its profit demands by establishing a relationship between the subject and the *beyond-the-pleasure principle*. With the symbol $, Lacan describes the access (which comes from language) of a fundamentally divided, incomplete, and inconsistent subject. In other words, the word "subject" cannot live up to what the symbol $ indicates since Lacan uses it to refer to a disappearing subject whose beginning is a traumatic rupture. This subject is never fully represented by the signifiers that enable its unstable emergence and position.

I consider that capitalist discourse reveals the neoliberal operation better than anything else since it establishes the connection between dominant power with a production of subjectivity given over to demands that exceed the subject constituted

DOI: 10.4324/9781003409410-2

by language, meaning that it turns out to be transformed into a being that some scholars of neoliberalism characterize as "human capital." Human capital does not mean simply the human being transformed into value/commodity, but it also refers to the place where the spheres belonging to the triad mourning-memory-desire are blocked and captured by distinct mechanisms, even though these experiences of the subject may be unable to be appropriated by *capitalist discourse* (see note at the end of this book). Those mechanisms promote unlimited growth, where the subject's surplus enjoyment finds itself always forced to return to the same place and initiate the cycle of reproduction – a cycle that slowly becomes the death drive.

When the assemblage of Fordist and industrial master discourse is completely eroded, so-called human capital or *homo economicus* emerges. Presented in Lacanian terms, I would say that the subject of the unconscious (issuing from the existence of language) is given over to profit demands specific to the structure of neoliberalism. Neoliberalism is not homeostatic, rather, it demands an energy that brings along unlimited growth beyond the pleasure principle. Ultimately, it is about eclipsing the subject in its symbolic possibilities in favor of a surplus enjoyment that subordinates it to a circuit of compulsion and repetition. To be clear, *homo economicus* can also be thought of from a political economy of pleasure perspective. In this perspective, I will affirm that Lacan's algebraic construction, the logical frame of capitalist discourse, turns out to be valid as a *matheme* for understanding neoliberalism. This matter corresponds to an era in which what Lacan called surplus enjoyment – symbolized with the letter (a) – is no longer simply exchanged between the $ and the Other of language. Surplus enjoyment simultaneously means a loss and a surplus of satisfaction, as much for the subject as for the Other. In the time of Lacan's capitalist discourse hypothesis, relative to this surplus enjoyment, surplus value is also metabolized, and the offerings of pleasure – directed to the Other in its religious, ritualistic, traditional variants organized by the master discourse – are now channeled by capitalist discourse.

Consequently, to begin sketching out what the era in which this pandemic realizes its deathly unfolding is like, I will refer to neoliberalism as being, of course, the "watchword" of the era. In geology, there exists a term "eon" which establishes a sort of iron law which gives place to and forms an era. In our era, we do not have the symbolic resources nor an imaginary alternative that would allow us to think about what comes after, presented as a rupture or a progressive transformation. This *impasse* continues to be crucial and determinative when it comes to thinking projects of emancipation, beyond the validity and the importance that those still have. In principle, one must accept the existence of a clear inability to symbolize and imagine a leftist transformative project, a radical or exterior outside, given capital's influence over the real – unless one thinks of it, like some social practices of self-organization, through "separate islands" that have generated an exchange logic and object to capitalist functioning. Nevertheless, beyond the inspiring character that these new ideological praxes can have, presenting them as a permanent alternative with respect to capitalism would constitute a phantasmatic solution. In any case, in their very existence, they demonstrate that capitalist reality is not an absolute that can close itself. This is, without a doubt, their most inspiring aspect. We are all children of this historical era conditioned by neoliberalism; for that reason, there are many authors who have taken up and developed this theme. In the pages that follow, I will signal some points that I consider relevant for elucidating the question of the current era and the pandemic, both in their political reach and subjective influences.

A)   Subject and Subjectivity

Foucault was the first thinker to put an important accent on the study of neoliberalism with his notion of biopolitics as a response to the difficulties that capitalism had (already in the 1970s) with finding forms of legitimation that would provide it a certain sustainability. The neoliberal solution to the problem of capitalism's cultural and political legitimation had to find the so-called "government of souls." Neoliberalism proposed itself as a shepherd whose goal was to unify the general command of power relationships with the distinct productions of subjectivity. These productions of subjectivity accomplish two simultaneous programs: on the one hand, there is always an instance that unifies them under the aegis of neoliberal domination, but at the same time, these subjectivities are presented in social life as animated by a fragmented, segmented, and determined mode both by fantasies and different ideologies.

The most distinct characteristic of neoliberalism consists in capturing and producing subjectivities in accordance with the unlimited reproduction of capitalism, which, even if they do not resolve its internal tensions, offer a territory in which they are configured, extinguished, and remade. For this reason, the crucial matter for neoliberalism is not smoothing out or reconciling its internal tensions but, rather, having them block the possible emergence of a possible project of transformation based on the construction of a subject that is able to intervene in its historical context. This blockage does not necessarily proceed from a vertical and repressive power, since the internal tensions are constitutively blocked by the very same mode in which they have been produced and by the symbolic horizon that they share – a horizon marked at every moment by the acceleration advanced by the rhythm of financial flows and, nevertheless, always returning to the same place in which capitalism propels itself.

Foucault already discerned that the unlimited capitalist machine, if it wanted to keep functioning, had to introduce itself into subjectivity, even redesigning it in order to continue. He was correct on this matter because, through the first two decades of the 21st century, neoliberalism has not stopped developing mechanisms, techniques, knowledges, strategies, and discourses that operate on the subject to tie together power and liberty in the society of control described by the French thinker. This continues today. In this aspect, neoliberalism is the mechanism that attempts to erase the subject in its singular existence as a speaking, sexuated, and mortal existence since it tries to substitute it for a subjectivity that aims always to be contemporary with itself. I often insist that we must distinguish the subject constituted by the symbolic Other (an empty subject, not identical to itself and eventually open to the cause of desire) from the relationships of power that produce the consumer-consumed subjectivity. Without this distinction, everything would remain entangled in power relationships, and it would become impossible to determine where one might subtract oneself from them. For example, a contra-hegemonic experience of constituting oneself as such would always be done starting from the subject and not from subjectivity. I should note, however, that on various occasions, Judith Butler has objected to this position. For Butler, in their critique of Lacan relative to the erasure of the subject, it should not be considered as a "transcendental a priori." For the US philosopher, the bar that erases the subject – indicator of its inconsistency and non-completion – should be understood as an effect of domination, historically constructed. In Butler's reading, this bar would obstruct the subject's displacement in new and distinct historical contexts, in this way being able to choose new sexual identities that were repressed in the historical sequence in which the bar was produced. But for Lacan, the bar is structural and irreducible; it never erases the subject's distinct and possible choices. The subject can identify as queer, trans, and other modalities, but that would never cancel the radical division of itself since that division would continue operating in those identifications, and the subject would have to decide how to know what to do with it.

To be specific, the place where the subjectivities produced by neoliberalism's various mechanisms are always found is in the relationships of domination. Perhaps this distinction (which in many cases has not been made by Foucault's followers) explains why his personal assistant, François Ewald, interprets his teacher in a neoliberal key, which today would make one think of Ewald as a distant predecessor of those libertarians who interpret pandemic confinement as an imposition of power. In this way, we observe that the measures taken by different governments around the world to control the coronavirus have been interpreted by these citizens as an affront to "their" freedom. In the different marches that proliferated around the world by the so-called "pandemic-deniers," we saw a curious metamorphosis. The government impositions taken to contain the lethal reach of the virus were understood as power grabs against which one must rise up. At the same time, this libertarian uprising against public health measures conceals its reverse: an extreme servitude to the market so that it can continue its functioning, with no attention paid to its disastrous effects.

We must remember that, upon leaving behind his famous *repressive hypothesis* since it could not account for the real operations of power, Foucault began to think about the society of control in which the prison walls would begin to be blurred. Nevertheless, neoliberalism has inaugurated a new stage of incarceration: prison camps, refugee camps, and immigrant camps that criminalize precarious sectors excluded from the symbolic camp, where experiences that order life could be transmitted. On the other hand, some feminist philosophers who follow Foucault (Nancy Fraser, Wendy Brown, and the aforementioned Judith Butler), when considering the political problem and analyzing the enormous inequalities produced by neoliberalism, do not neglect its punitive factor. This is an aspect that Foucault, in his biopolitical reflections, did not take up sufficiently. In any case, neoliberalism is a sort of absolutism that should not be confused with the historical totalitarianism of the 20th century, which were not based explicitly on the capture of subjectivity, even if they had similar aspirations. I say absolutism because neoliberalism truly attempts a total appropriation that tries to erase the constitutive differences and orienting fictions of democratic space.

B)   May '68 Capture

The government of souls originating from neoliberalism has led to a subjectivity that reveals itself as separate from all the symbolic coordinates that we used to know. Capitalist subjectivity is constructed such that, in it, historical legacies are not recognized, and it unfolds in an absolute present without understanding nor wanting to know anything about political projects. This absolute present also threatens the implicit temporality in the singular history of each one of us – temporality that I describe using the Lacanian formula: *what I will have been for what I am in the process of becoming.* For neoliberalism, however, existence has to play in the absolute present and, in this way, be remitted to the circulation of "novelties." Novelty is the signature of the absolute present. Because of this, it is necessary to differentiate the "new" as an incalculable and unforeseeable contingency from the iterative circuit of novelties. The new that remits to the new conceals the compulsion to repetition. Even projects that are inaugurated with a decidedly emancipatory aim can be integrated into the "avarice of novelties." A key example of the way in which neoliberalism can include critical thought in the mercantile circuit of the novel was May 1968. Early on, the premises of '68, as is known, gave form to a new spirit of capitalism. The new Master began to privilege new initiatives, original talent, imagination, and creativity, as long as it all organized itself through market order, of course.

The students of '68 had violently traversed the fantasy of progress and had captured the inconsistency that the symbolic Other embodied in reality. In this way, '68 made a "non-knowledge" emerge over social ties. For this reason, the revolt was possible and introduced an ethico-political crisis unprecedented in Europe. But there was still a coming Master: the capitalist discourse that was going to carry out a distinct operation. While the lack appears in a synchronous time, it is also filled to the brim with the presence of an object, which, at the same time, renews the dissatisfaction of the desire. On this point, we can evoke the moment in which Lacan, in the Panthéon of Paris, directed himself to the students and said something revealing to them: "Do you want a master? You will have one." And it was precisely the new master of the market that irrupted in order to dominate and satiate the chants of '68, chants like, "All power to the imagination!" or "Bee realistic, demand the impossible!" It is true that the master which the students called upon did not have traditional support, and neither was it linked to historical legacies. Perhaps because of this, the protesters could not foresee that, effectively, capitalism's renovation needed neoliberal discourses to be able to produce that desire in the subject, to be able to incorporate it in terms of liberty. This translation of May '68 can give an account of capitalist discourse's capacity, in its circularity, to reintegrate what was presented as a rupture and a new cycle into a new transformation.

In a similar sense, we can understand that the protesters against pandemic confinement felt themselves to be "libertarian" when, in reality, what they were doing was voluntarily serving capitalism's advance. When, with their demand for "liberty," they told themselves that they were being coerced under a dictatorial power, they were really favoring the Caudine Forks of the market. In a certain way, neoliberalism has been successful in trapping many elements that both traditional conservative and liberal thought have not been able to reabsorb. This was the reason for their distinct crises of legitimacy. This was resolved with the configuration of a subjectivity that operates as an ally of capitalism in which crises, instead of debilitating its movement, do nothing else but relaunch it, fortifying its structure of domination. For all of these reasons, it was confirmed long ago that capitalism tends toward a new type of state of exception. What used to require a classical military coup now displaces and condenses itself in power constituted by a conglomerate of corporations, financial groups, and international connections, whose novelty resides in reaching – at least partially – a new psychic apparatus. As I have already affirmed on various occasions, this gives dominant ideology a form of penetration into the phantasmatic order (and vice versa) that sustains the subject in its reality. In the subjectivity produced by capitalism, the ideological interpellation described by Althusser inscribes itself in the demands of the super-ego specific to neoliberal time. We have to remember that the destruction of diverse identificatory groups (like popular sectors, community groups, or families) does not only reduce the lethal potential of the super-ego but, rather, amplify it.

C) Output and Depression

One of neoliberalism's most powerful strategies consists in getting subjectivity to surrender to output, the life of the subject being governed by fierce competition. This provokes a libidinal change. In this way, the potentiality of neoliberalism implies that existential experiences like love and sexuality no longer find a place where they can unfold via social ties, as an adventure between the different entanglements that arise in the always problematic relationship between love, desire, and pleasure. The worldwide extension of depression (even prior to the pandemic) is, in this way, shown to be an effect achieved by neoliberalism. Depression, which is always a resignation in the face of desire and its avatars, is no longer presented solely as a mental pathology but, rather, as one of the contemporary manifestations of subjectivity production. Even the celebrated "self-entrepreneur" would be a figure stripped of the ethical duties of desire, being substituted, instead, for different types of performances: capital, sexual-erotic, or sport. These transactions, always unlimited, will sooner or later lock down the compulsive movement of a drive. If the death drive did so, then it would capture consciousness entirely. To be more precise, it would make consciousness its preferred erogenous zone by taking possession of it, would endow depressed existence with moral masochism and, as a consequence, the subject would live in permanent malaise for never measuring up.

All of this confirms that neoliberalism is an extraordinary producer of precarious life. Here, I use the expression in the same way that the philosopher José Luis Villacañas uses it, precarious life referring not only to the obvious vulnerability and exclusion of the popular or more subaltern sectors of society but, rather, as an expression whose reach is greater. This is because the exploiters also cannot have an authentic human life, being obligated to the maintenance of the unlimited reproduction of capital in a constant updating of primitive accumulation, now working alongside finance capital and the different operations of dispossession of raw materials in emerging nations. In other words, neoliberalism has been appropriating everything that makes an experience of the common possible (as a matter of fact, one of Lacan's theses expresses that capitalism, in its discursive construction, constitutes itself on a rejection of love, a rejection to which I add the common). Obviously, precarity does not do away with the antagonisms between oligarchies and the people, but thanks to the unifying power of neoliberalism which prevents one from thinking a way out, precarious life is becoming the essence of the great neoliberal creation – life entirely reduced to value, to competition between others, and also with respect to one's self. To understand the reach of this operation, we must insist on the double operation of capitalist discourse. On the one hand, it unifies life under a single impulse, but at the same time, this unification is only achieved, paradoxically, with the fragmentation of distinct social ties.

D) Debt and Superego

Neoliberalism is the era of capitalism whose accumulation model is no longer characterized solely by the exchange of commodities but also by credit and debt. One of its greatest novelties is made real in the fact that debt does not only penetrate into nations and their social fabrics, but, rather, it includes subjectivity as well. As a consequence, the relationship between creditor and debtor is inscribed in an order beyond the merely economic such that neoliberalism tends to be realized, as Maurizio Lazzarato would say based on his readings of Nietzsche and Deleuze, in a factory of debtors. In this way, singular existence is pressured to live under the logic of credit and debt. However, in my view – different from Lazzarato, for whom singular existence is pressured to unfold under the credit/debt logic – it is necessary to understand that neoliberalism can only have this capacity to capture if it touches a key element of the psychic apparatus: the superego. Without its necessary participation, the relationship of circular movement between renunciation and excess could not be established like it is in capitalist discourse. A reciprocal play between that which the subject always lacks and the promises of novelties that could satisfy said lack is produced. The subject renounces immediate satisfaction but cannot liberate themselves from the compulsion that admonishes them to satisfy it. The more important the renunciation, the more it stains itself, compulsively, with unconscious feelings of guilt because the renunciation never satisfies the appetite of the superegoic creditor, who always demands more and more. In this same logic of debt, we can understand both the mandates of the International Monetary Fund (IMF) (this is clearly observed in countries that have been captured by debt – whatever they may do, they must always pay more) as well as the subject's most intimate duties which are co-opted by the obscene voracity of the superego. Freud compared the unconditioned character of this voracity with Kant's categorical imperative. Lacan then showed the sadistic opposite of that Law: it demands pleasure instead of prohibiting. Under this logic, the subject conceives existence itself outside of any historical link, and as a consequence, it becomes depoliticized or inscribed in a rejection of politics. As a result, the very ones who engendered the debt end up benefiting.

The subject, as Freud, Heidegger, and Lacan explain, arrives in the world guilty and as a debtor due to its constitutive structure. For the first time, neoliberalism has proven able to colonize that originary instance of the subject by setting the market operation onto the construction of subjectivity – a subjectivity that is oriented towards the substitution of political life in favor of the constraints of survival. Emphasis is usually put on the joyful and incessant consumption of objects, but it is in the compulsive and repetitive character where the dark death drive remains hidden, and its always possible translation to the privileged channel of hatred. In our era – the pandemic era governed by neoliberalism – it is more and more difficult to decide what a life not regulated by the superegoic balances between success and failure would be like. Also, in this context, we can understand that various contemporary far-rights are a sort of emanation of neoliberalism's new death drive since, if they spoke plainly, they might say something like the following: "Since you will never escape the threatening and sinister logic, we offer you the chance to be on the sadistic side of the punishers." For neoliberalism, the matter is not primarily about toppling leftist, nationalist, or populist governments, but mainly about making the threatening logic permeate into even the most remote corners of a community. Its essential purpose is, thus, to position democracy itself under its own control.

E) Shame

Among the feelings that neoliberalism has disrupted is shame, which, alongside shyness, is a veil that reveals that one does not find one's self totally dominated by the most obscene interests that give rein to the pure enjoyment of accumulation. As I have indicated elsewhere, what currently governs is not only the accumulation of enjoyment but also the very compulsion of enjoyment not yet accumulated and that others pay for said compulsion with their sacrifice. The problem is to see how it would traverse the indolent barbarism of the representatives of the oligarchy who spread irresponsible hate. We are witnessing a spectacle never before seen in democracy in which numerous shameless figures parade themselves around in the political sphere with unlimited impunity. This could eventually become the formal beginning of the collapse of our civilization. On this subject, paraphrasing Freud, we could ask: "What is the amount of death drive that a civilization can allow without its foundations being undermined?"

For years, under the "theological" dominion of neoliberalism, political space has been invaded by personalities completely dominated by their narcissist drives, those that, in a fight for pure prestige, make death the absolute Master. Just like we used to speak of the "authoritarian personality" with regards to National Socialism, now neoliberal reason requires "characters" who embody megalomania, hatred, and destructive narcissism. This can no longer be understood in terms of Hannah Arendt's famous notion of the "banality of evil" but, rather, constitutes a new and dangerous form of the evil of banality. I am referring to a destructive drive that, while it is indeed tied to the demands of capitalist reproduction, adds a supplementary extra, a series of procedures that can be put in service of espionage and population control and which exceed the specific utility of intelligence services. Rather, they promote a pure, sadistic exercise of narcissistic identification that not only aims to justify itself under a simulacrum of "democracy" but also claims victimhood while it does damage. This new knot between pathology, subjectivity, and politics should be considered in order to understand how the current megalomania of so many political figures has been possible and sustained by a consensus that, on occasion, has tied itself to social madness in its most paranoid aspects, as this new era where narcissist and destructive governors have become common currency shows. Even though they may later fail in their electoral projects or effective governments, they leave an inertia in society that sediments itself in the social fabric. Now, we do not need to analyze the actions of that type of character from the perspectives of cognitive sciences or neurosciences – psychology or psychiatry – because, in my view, their acts do not respond to mental-organic pathologies but, rather, are required by a structural necessity of neoliberalism that, for its own sustainability, requires leaders with sufficient impunity and irresponsibility.

Neoliberalism especially needs subjects with an insubstantial and parodic character to embody the headless dimension characteristic of the capitalism of our time. Ultimately, the neoliberal command dictates that they work in the same social space and at the same time – both the economic march for corporations and the policy for narcissists in the service of pure conspiracy of hate, even if they do not always rule. Here we find a structural limit, since the market is not sure in its operations, because, in principle, they must try to extend themselves to the entire population, including the precarious, the marginalized, and the oppressed. In this regard, while I have insisted that the extreme right has already intervened in the agenda of the classical and conservative right, it should also be noted that, for now, that is not the place where the market feels comfortable in its deployment. Because capitalist discourse demands the inclusion of almost everyone in this capture, and the extreme right, with its segregative logic is the best instrument for it. That is why they only function as plan B, as a pure intimidating exercise so that progressive, national, or popular democratic governments perceive, according to the different conjunctures, a force that pressures them, even though when governing they are replaced by better-disguised rights with a democratic face.

F)   Möbius Strip

Given the circular movement of capitalist discourse, I am going to attempt a representation of it, parting from the famous Escher's Möbius strip in which an ant always travels across the same surface. The feature of the one-sided band, as its name indicates, is that it does not have two surfaces. This allows us to understand the difficulties presented when attempting to make a cut into capitalist discourse. There is no *a priori* site from which to make an "anti-capitalist" cut. For example, if we made a sharp, transversal cut across the band, it would break, meaning that by presenting itself as pure destruction, it would lack any political representation of itself. This would imply thinking that the functioning of capitalism would be destroyed if chaos and disaster were produced, and in that way, it would lose its capacity to reproduce itself endlessly in circular movement. Dismissing the transversal cut, then, we could attempt a longitudinal cut through the middle, but by doing so, we would only achieve a bilateral band that would lose its Möbius character.

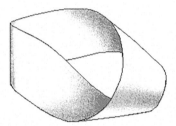

Figure 1.1 – möbius strip

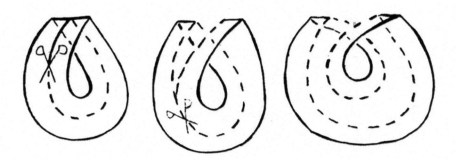

Figure 1.2 – three strips, cuts

Longitudinal cut through the middle.

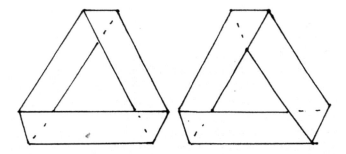

Figure 1.3 – two strips, triangle

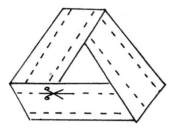

Figure 1.4 – one strip, triangle with cuts

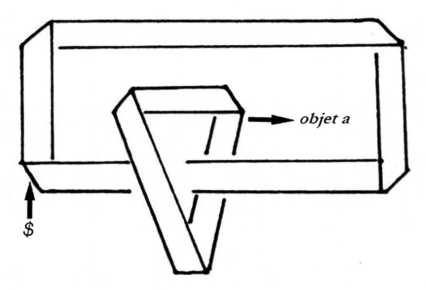

Figure 1.5 – one strip (triangle) joined to another (rectangle)

My proposal is to make a longitudinal cut into thirds.

If we make a longitudinal cut into thirds, not only do we not destroy the Möbius strip, but the cut also obtains a new, unilateral strip that is tied to the rest, operations by which Lacan topologically illustrates both the division of the subject, $\math$, and the object (a).

The enigmatic condition of the attempt to translate this proposed cut into politics is not lost on me. Different from those who propose that there can be an absolute cut that might give rise to something exterior to capitalist discourse, here I propose a more arduous path. This path implies making a longitudinal cut into thirds. This cut, in principle, is interior to capitalist discourse, but in it, nevertheless, two elements that the functioning of capitalist discourse has rejected are obtained: the division of the subject and the object that causes desire. Given that the representations of possible exits from capitalist discourse are extremely problematic, here I will allow myself to venture this peculiar mode of non-completeness of the same: a cut that, again, gives place to the $\math$ division of the subject and the object that causes desire (a), which capitalist discourse had sealed with *plus de jouir*; a relationship with the cause of desire, which cannot happen in capitalist discourse. The metaphor of the longitudinal cut into thirds allows us to show that the exit from capitalism is more related to a political construction that cuts it longitudinally from within and from a determined place (the third). At the same time, this construction cannot integrate the remains that operate as a cause through any sort of dialectical mediation. For this reason, in principle, the exit is always partial and contingent.

Chapter 2

No-politics

With the neologism no-politics, I refer to a modality where politics no longer has an anchor. This absence of an anchor point is one of the effects achieved by the workings of capitalist discourse. This discourse, being governed by the mechanism that Lacan isolated in psychosis under the name foreclosure, is characterized by the destruction of the quilting point (*point de capiton*), the site where the relationship between signifier and signified is stabilized. In other words, signifiers do not slide along an infinite chain thanks to those anchoring points that make possible a retroactive signification. Recall processes always demand an anchoring point, given that when one is foreclosed, an infinite delusional drift emerges. In the case of no-politics, the absence of an anchoring point is compensated by the proliferative activity of the media apparatuses and social networks, which, ultimately, are manifested in a series of accusations, fake news, and rumors that are, themselves, contradictory and contradict others. All of these media powers constitute a serious obstacle to political operations that, by definition, always demand the stabilization of certain signifiers. The transversal expansion of no-politics is one of the main obstacles that political action encounters in contemporary praxis. It follows from this that the efficiency of fake news and its possible distortions may not find its true base of support in lies about reality, but, rather, that they have a more efficient structural means in which both ideology and the ghost of the subject are implicated. Without an anchoring point, an experience of the truth is suspended and moves towards an unlimited drift where the relationship with historical legacies is canceled.

This era, as I have been saying, is no longer about the threatening logic developed in the classic dictatorships nor in the logic promoted by despotic and totalitarian absolutisms. The threatening logic now proceeds in an invisible and perhaps imperceptible way, arriving at a climax in moments of widespread catastrophe, as we have seen with the Covid-19 pandemic. At the same time, it is not about the terror exposed in the Leviathan that, at any moment, can make us feel its violence, rather, it has to do with systemic and uncanny violence that entails being trapped in a circular movement that always returns to the same site. While there may be pandemics, insurrections, ecological catastrophes, crises of representation, the bursting of financial bubbles, etc. – despite all of this, neoliberalism remains.

DOI: 10.4324/9781003409410-3

A threatening logic appears to run through humanity. We are not able to view a possible exit from this circularity in which large-scale, transformative human experiences appear impossible in both an existential and political sense. This threatening logic, however, may be the key to insisting on the possibility of emancipation. It is when the fear that comes over subjects (due to their thrownness without any protection) becomes anguish that the space of anticipatory resolutions and, perhaps, the decisions that wake us up are opened. In these cases, the real question is if the passage from fear to the authenticity of anguish and its decision can find a political translation that points toward true emancipation at the right time.

Chapter 3

The Uncanny

The uncanny is the psychic base of the threatening logic. Because of this, I consider it very important to understand its internal structure. Here, I will allow myself a brief gloss of Freud's text *Das Unheimliche* (*The Uncanny*), which gives an account of this experience. The internal atmosphere of the text is already very contaminated by what will later become one of Freud's fundamental works, *Beyond the Pleasure Principle*, where he will give a radical turn with respect to its prior development by establishing that the original principle of the unconscious is not the pleasure principle but, rather, its beyond, which implies incorporating the compulsion to repetition and the death drive as protagonists of the structure of the unconscious. From that moment, the unconscious becomes denser, darker, and more inert. In this context, we can understand precisely the reach that the uncanny has in the psychic apparatus.

Freud begins with a surprising invitation by considering the uncanny as an aesthetic category, which alters the very root of the traditional conception of the theory of the beautiful. Keeping in mind that Freud has always been especially discrete in his relationship to traditional philosophy, this text stands out in the way that it confronts Schelling's definition: "Unheimlich is the name for everything that ought to have remained secret and hidden but has come to light." In his response to Schelling, Freud submerges himself – almost as if he were a Heidegger or Derrida *avant la lettre* – in crowd of German language voices extracted from a flowery literary heritage by going over poems, texts, stories, and certain declensions that allow him to explain what, for him, will be the essential characteristic of the uncanny. For Freud, the uncanny does not emerge from the encounter with something new or merely strange, not even from the unclassifiable. On the contrary, the condition of being "familiar" is what makes the uncanny possible. This is because it appears as an element that is simultaneously exterior and intimate, being a phenomenon that overflows into and invades the interior of the everyday by interrupting it with its disquieting strangeness. In this way, when the uncanny presents itself, the semblances of the familiar begin to break down. From here, the disruptive character, the sudden emergence, that the uncanny can have is understood.

Freud carries out an excellent philological investigation, specifically with the etymologies of the word uncanny, and highlights a strange and very peculiar linguistic

DOI: 10.4324/9781003409410-4

sleight of hand since the antonyms *Heim* (familiar) and *Unheim* (uncanny) end up being equivalents. In this way, Freud manages to do something similar to an echo chamber with words, giving place for them to articulate themselves in a fine-tuned resonance, producing a very curious and relevant effect: antonym becomes synonym. In summary, the essential problematic centers on knowing what Schelling wanted to say with the enigmatic sentence: "Everything that ought to have remained secret and hidden but has come to light." If the uncanny is a part of the familiar, we can affirm, then, already in Freudian terms, that the familiar is the privileged site where the uncanny returns.

However, Freud does not dedicate himself solely to philology. He considers that linguistic analysis is insufficient and realizes that it is necessary to put the structure of the unconscious into play – something which is entirely absent in Schelling. In his analysis, the return of the repressed, the repetition compulsion, and castration anxiety participate in the experience of the uncanny. The articulation of those three concepts, in their logical operation, will once again allow Freud to roll out and understand the functioning of psychic structure. In Freud, what routinely appears as an anomalous fact becomes, in the end, that which ends up explaining the structure of the unconscious. In this case, we have to differentiate between the return of the repressed and the repetition compulsion because both mechanisms are engaged in the emergence of the experience of the uncanny. The return of the repressed forms part of the symbolic order – what Lacan will call the order of the signified – which explains how the echo chamber these terms exist in implies the outcome where antonym becomes synonym. Conversely, the repetition compulsion is linked to drive, as Freud explains in *Beyond the Pleasure Principle*, where he even refers to the "destiny" of the subject.

The return of the repressed is not something that has happened nor something traumatic that the subject repressed only for it to return. For Freud, the return of the repressed is never an event that has happened in the past and returned, but, rather, that repression, being structurally constitutive of the subject, organizes the distinct modes of reading the past by making history the site where the repressed can always reappear. The symbolic order is never sufficient for representing the real in its totality (for structural reasons), so there will always be repression and return of the repressed, thus provoking the effect of the uncanny. It is important to note that although Freud does say at the start of the text, as a narrative strategy, that he has no personal experience with the uncanny, giving the corresponding aesthetic indication, halfway through, we find the story of his famous experience in an Italian town with the "painted women," to use his expression. There he found himself circling again and again, seeking a way to leave the neighborhood, only to realize something important: he was always passing through the same spot. Only Freud is capable of splitting hairs in an experience of anxiety such as this, understanding that compulsion and repetition always accompany the uncanny. It is not until later work that he makes the connection between compulsion, repetition, and the return of the repressed. Lacan will then continue this thread and explain that, while these three categories are structural operations of the unconscious, one concerns the aspect of the signifier and the other its drive.

Referring to Ernst Theodor Amadeus Hoffman's story, "The Sandman" (where an analogy between the loss of one's eyes and the loss of an organ is established), Freud introduces the concept of castration anxiety. While Freud relates the uncanny with castration anxiety, since all the materials of the uncanny function as a metaphor for castration, what stands out is that castration anxiety does not constitute a real threat because he understands castration in relation to those objects that have been subtracted from imaginary and symbolic representation in the very constitution of the subject. This subtraction is no anomaly because the subject can never represent the real – essentially, the real of their body – except in a failed mode. What the subject can capture of its body, through image or through signifiers, will never be the totality of their body since it is "lacking." In this way, perhaps we can understand that castration anxiety, as an initial experience, is already indicative of the fact that there are certain elements that are subtracted from the logic of representation and that, by reappearing, they always puncture the subject's world.

Heidegger also alludes to the uncanny in his existential analytic described in *Being and Time*. It is worth it to dwell on the possible reach of a potential link between Freud and Heidegger on this matter. Lacan thinks that, in *Being and Time*, alongside Freud, one of the biggest subversions of the Cartesian subject and Kantian transcendental subject emerges. As is known, Heidegger attempts to think *Dasein*, factic life, and he critiques philosophers who have not taken up the singularity of *Dasein*. Of course, his extensive analysis gives an account of being towards death, not sexuality. Still, in Lacanian terms, we can understand castration as "being towards death" and give the name "drive object" to the void that the drive traverses. This can, at the same time, assimilate with Heidegger's "nothingness," because Heidegger needs to use terms like "concealment" and "avoidance," which, in my view, do not give an account of what type of operations sustains them. When we read *Being and Time* from a Lacanian perspective, we frequently have the sense that Heidegger carries out an unexpected analysis of the unconscious because the subject covers up, does not want to know anything, hides, or tries to do everything possible to ignore its lack of foundation. Nevertheless, it is never possible to grasp what would be the structural operation that sets up and causes the avoidance effect. Neither is it clear what would be the reasons why the subject would not want to know anything about all of this. On this matter, Freud can be read as a response to Heidegger, and this is precisely what Lacan did.

In Heidegger, the subject lives in impropriety, between rumors, between saying-this and saying-that, what Heidegger calls "the one of rumors." In this sense, we can understand that there is an improper or inauthentic origin of *Dasein*. It turns out that "there" is when one understands one's self as thrown into the world, lacking foundation, without anything to justify one's self, and it is then when the experience of anxiety can begin. In this ontological analytic of anxiety, Heidegger sees in "being thrown" an inevitable moment, being that of the uncanny, which is translated as "not being home" or "the inhospitable." In other words, *Dasein* lived among gossip, machinations, and rumors, and therein lies its impropriety. The mortal being begins to understand what is at stake for its own life precisely when it encounters its own abyss, its lack of foundation and uprootedness. As opposed to Nietzsche, Heidegger discerned that the *Übermensch* was not someone strong, beyond good and bad. Rather, he conceived of them as a stupid boxer in charge of the State, absolutely devoid of the horizon where the difference between being and entity could illuminate a new light in existence. After his infamous episode as rector in Freiburg, he sensed that the will to power gave way to arrogant, overblown morons, wholly dominated by the worldwide order of *technē* and its machinations. On this point, the enormous number of neo-fascist madmen that swarm around our society of the spectacle appears to confirm his hypothesis. This reading of Nietzsche's will to power brings Heidegger to think that its exercise would lead to a sad ending for the human race since, impotent, it would drown "in the frozen waters of selfish calculus." From there, he proposes another beginning.

Now, a hundred years later, we say that Heidegger already saw that uprooting was one of the consequences of *technē*. In this globalized era, its devastating effects have extended to the entire planet by implementing a generalized uprooting that has destroyed singularity, among other catastrophic effects of *technē*. From there we can imagine that Heidegger would see our present time as a world inhabited by uprooted zombies because no one is in a position to make anxiety an existential experience. This massive uprooting, caused by capitalist globalization, has produced a collapse that traps us and makes us lose the singular condition of foundationless experience. Along this slope, it is as if the uncanny has taken possession of the world and has lost the opportunity to pass to another.

This abyss, or the "not being at home," can lead us to think of others that are not at home either – refugees, immigrants, exiles – whose experience is radically different from the not being at home of singular existence. They emerge from an uprooting factory that annuls the possibility of constituting not being at home as a singular and originary experience. These groups are not afforded the existential experience of not being at home since this can only be experienced by those who do. Let's be clear on this paradoxical formulation. Just like someone who is in a concentration camp cannot have the experience of "being towards death," neither can those who are expelled from the world have the experience of not being at home described in Heidegger's existential analytic because one must have a world in order to experience not being at home. It seems to me that the inhospitable state of not being at home (*Unheimlich*) that Heidegger refers to is, rather, the condition that provides access to having an authentic life of one's own. On this matter, it is worth noting that, for Heidegger, the uncanny does not have a negative nuance since it ends up being the condition of possibility so that *Dasein*, when it finds itself in the moment of bankruptcy, can discover the possibility of its wager and resolution. In fact, for Heidegger, the uncanny constitutes an inevitable passage of *Dasein* which appears, in principle, distinct from Freud's position according to which, as

I have said, the uncanny is translated as clinical anxiety and not as destiny or an existential adventure. However, there is another possible reading of Freud's text because if the experience of the uncanny depends on a return of the repressed, then there occurs, in the subject, a lifting of the repression and, therefore, an opening to the possibilities offered by the unconscious – opening up to new senses, beyond symptomatic fixation and its compulsions that kept it closed.

In Freud's text, he presents the materials of the uncanny: orthopedic pieces, robots, and inanimate dolls that suddenly come to life. We must begin from the starting point that all of these materials of the uncanny call into question the unity of the self. They express the division of the subject since they show it to be split in all its radicality; even the figure of the double, who could have been sympathetic (an other who is similar to me and fascinates me from a narcissistic point of view), transforms into an intrusion by someone else occupying my place. This theme of the double is also one of the key materials of the uncanny. For example, when I look in the mirror, a strangeness is produced because I do not recognize myself in the other in the mirror. (This is precisely what psychoanalysis considers the site from which the child establishes the real basis of their narcissism.) From a Lacanian perspective, we can think of what we designate as *schizia*, the neologism invented by Lacan that alludes to the division or fracture between vision and gaze. That is to say, we must remember that, for Lacan, while vision is governed by geometrical objects, gaze, on the other hand, proceeds from the other, giving rise to a rupture between vision and gaze. In this way, we can affirm that the materials of the uncanny are constituted as such because "they gaze upon us," even though this specific aspect is not taken up in Freud's text. In any case, both in the figure of the double and in the orthopedic pieces and the eyes of the doll, what we see does not coincide with what gazes back. The materials of the uncanny acquire their libidinal value and condense it to the extent that they present themselves to us as objects that shelter the gaze. The uncanny is not only that which, being hidden, reveals itself; rather, it also gazes upon us, and it is there where the complete effect of the uncanny is truly realized. It is in this operation where it is revealed that the uncanny makes a cut in the veil that covers the real.

In his book *Lo bello y lo siniestro* (*The Beautiful and the Uncanny*), philosopher Eugenio Trías also analyzes this theme. In this book, he also prefigures his later "philosophy of the limit." On this point, we should remember that, by limit, he understands a border that joins and separates heterogeneous and asymmetrical fields, meaning he never refers to it as something merely negative by not thinking of it as a sort of red light that establishes a barrier or endpoint. Therefore, in the aforementioned text, when addressing the category of the beautiful, Trías situates it in relationship to the uncanny in order to elaborate his aesthetic theory. The author analyzes various themes that end in his study of the film *Vertigo* (one of his great obsessions to which he will return from different angles on numerous occasions). What is important to highlight about his aesthetics is this affirmation: there is no beauty if it does not have the very dimension of the uncanny as both cause and generating condition. Beauty is not only the uncanny's veil; the uncanny is also the cause of beauty. There is no work of art that is realized as such if it does not have some kind of metonymic relationship with the uncanny, hidden or as an "indicator."

On this point, post-Freudians charged that Freud's theories of the death drive, compulsion, repetition, and the eternal return of the same were influences of the war; they wanted to call Freud a pessimist. It was, on the contrary, the other way around. Freud presents the necessary theoretical elements so that war can be thought. In this way, war did not have, for him, an affective influence, but, rather, he decided to interrogate war deeply and arrive at the final consequences.

This development of the question in Freud can be pertinent to make more intelligible the uncanny character of the circular movement of capitalism: the return to the same place executed by neoliberal discourse.

Chapter 4

Evil

In order to analyze possible political ethics, I will now consider a difficult matter referred to by Kant in various texts: radical evil. As is well known, in his critique, he establishes that reason is the pure or transcendental faculty only in its practical dimension, limited as it is, not in its theoretical use. Practical reason or supreme will is autonomous, free, and unconditioned, and it gives itself moral law: the categorical imperative, the foundation, and a priori universal principle. This "holy" will – in the Kantian sense – is good when it works independently of all experience. I want to fulfill this duty out of respect for the fundamental moral law of pure reason, irrespective of any condition or experience. From there, the freedom of will would be that which produces the highest good, a priori. On the other hand, evil, in the strict sense, cannot be wanted unless we are dealing with a diabolic being. Kant understands the origin of evil as a subordination of reason to particular inclinations or versions (hatred, greed, envy, domination, etc.). As a consequence, evil is not something atemporal but, rather, historical, being related to the customs of concrete actors. In this way, evil is not considered a radical principle since it refers to the vulgar or ordinary. In other words, evil opposes the concept of the highest good (horizon of the synthesis between liberty and nature, the end of will) that has to do with "humanity." This horizon is never fully reached and maintains an "asymptomatic" relationship in the geometrical sense, in a line that, indefinitely prolonged, gets progressively closer to a curve but never fully finds it.

For Kant, good and evil are not compatible, but goodwill in general is one thing, and evil, which comes from the frailty of human nature, is another. On this point, we could establish a possible analogy with Freud because his theory does not suppose a divided cosmogony between two drives – life and death – by understanding that in the drive itself, each organism "wants to die in its own way." Therefore, there is no compatibility between life and death drives, although it could happen that the death drive presents itself as a rupture in the habitual channels of its circuit and destroys desire since death drive refers to an irreducible excess present in the different drives that only operates as deadly enjoyment when the radical experience of desire and love leave it room.

As has been said, for Kant, evil does not constitute an a priori principle because it depends on the inclinations of human nature. It can, on the other hand, appear

DOI: 10.4324/9781003409410-5

as an obstacle so that singular will obeys moral law. Practical reason is transcendental, nonetheless; its autonomous exercise as supreme will is conditioned by human frailty, which does not tend towards the good. In this way, the attainment of freedom turns out to be out of reach. Freud does not accept the opposition between "the pathological" conditioned by particular interest and the metaphysical foundation of morality. In his analysis, the categorical imperative and the functioning of the superego are structurally linked, understanding that consciousness's voice carries coercion that gives rise to the feeling of unconscious guilt. Paradoxically, for Freud, in the renunciation of immediate pleasure, a "beyond" operates in which the subject enjoys their own renunciation in a superegoic way.

Given all of this, we can ask: is evil a political category? Or should it stay in the order of the moral-theological? These questions have become legitimate in our era, where the demands of capitalist discourse aim to erase the difference between the death drive and the insistence on the cause of desire. Here, the key point is to distinguish between that insistence and the repetition compulsion. One must save desire from repetition compulsion since that would imply that desire, even though it may not be definitively freed from death drive, would offer a possible path towards realization if it passed through the symbolic Other. Now, this path should not be intercepted by the compulsive logic of consumption. On the contrary, I believe that the experience of love, in a Lacanian sense, occurs as the possibility of living outside the logic of the market. This experience has nothing to do with a mere exchange of benefits or a pact exclusively referring to the enjoyment of the *partenaires* since love, even though it is reciprocal, should be traversed by the exercise of a free gift.

Chapter 5

Fantasy
Ideology

In order to understand the questions I have been developing in relation to our era, I think it important to analyze the problematic relationship between fantasy and ideology, even though this theme deserves a deeper and more extensive study. In any case, here I will focus on some relevant ideas. Taking Louis Althusser as a reference, I have carried out a critical commentary on his celebrated text "Ideology and Ideological State Apparatus (Notes Towards an Investigation)" in order to establish a relationship between these two operations which implicate the subject in their constant and habitual experiences. The prominent place I give to the French thinker is due to the fact that we have, in his texts, the first encounter between a general theory of ideology (following the Marxist tradition) and Lacanian postulates about the subject. In this sense, I have tried to maintain the inaugural tension between fantasy and ideology to show their border relationship, conjunction, and disjunction, in which both places sustain and attract each other.

My proposal differs from that of Slavoj Žižek, perhaps the most well-known commentator on ideology, who has established a homology between fantasy and ideology by superimposing or covering them through expressions like ideological fantasy or ideology of the unconscious. On this subject, and on different occasions, Žižek investigates the fantasy of antisemitism and analyzes, in the figure of the rejected and excluded object, its important role in the functioning of the "ideological fantasy" since it ensures that reality stands as such. In this way, both fantasy and ideology form part of the frame within which reality is represented, on the condition that there always be an excluded remainder, both exterior and interior, but essential for sustaining that reality, understood from a Lacanian perspective.

In the second place, my proposal also differs from that of the Essex School, which waters down the terms fantasy and ideology under the term hegemonic logic. In effect, Ernesto Laclau, one of its greatest exponents, develops this line of thought and clarifies the political efficacy of specific signifiers in the construction of hegemonic logic, distancing it from the problem of ideology. For Laclau, what is important is analyzing how a partial and differential element, through a discursive construction, becomes the representative of the totality. In that way, the question of the "discursive construction" substitutes the problem linked to the themes of fantasy and ideology.

DOI: 10.4324/9781003409410-6

While we could establish many differences between ideology and fantasy in terms of their different modes of operation, it is also true that both operations possess a family resemblance, as Wittgenstein would say, to the extent that they constitute the system of representations that governs the relationship of the subject to the real. In this perspective, we must differentiate between reality and the real from the start. For Lacan, the real is impossible. It designates a hole in reality where anxiety, trauma, nightmares, death drive, the uncanny, or absolute violence burst in: that which cannot be symbolized in its totality. On the other hand, the term reality makes reference to the sum of fantasy and ideology mechanisms that protect the subject by giving them the distance that allows them to stabilize themselves in relation to the impossible real. We will see how Althusser did not have this distinction in mind, and that, in my view, it is essential to confront the theme of fantasy/ideology.

The fantasy/ideology problem is enormously relevant for two reasons. On the one hand, it is relevant because it concerns the very constitution of the subject, and on the other, because it also influences the social field in a time like ours where there are more and more phenomena that have introduced phantasmatic elements in the same social structure and in the evolution of the political, which should no longer be interpreted, in the classical way, as mere ideological phenomena. Without a doubt, these different phantasmatic signs, which spontaneously present themselves in current times and are manifested in multiple situations, have become very relevant. For example, one can be ideologically feminist and, at the same time, have rape or submission fantasies; a worker can be on the progressive left from the social point of view and, at the same time, show themselves to be extremely reactionary in other spheres of life, positioning themselves against the diversity of sexual roles, against homosexuality and same-sex marriage, etc.

At stake is the attempt to answer questions such as what relationship can be established between fantasy and ideology? What class of orders or realities are designated by these categories? Or also, how do they operate, and in what way are they distributed? In what follows, I will break down some essential points where I attempt to give an answer to this problematic relationship between fantasy and ideology. Both operations constitute an order – a combinatorial or a structuring order – of representations that govern how, particularly paradoxically, the subject is related to reality.

A)   The Althusserian Turn

In Althusser's text, many of us in Argentina discovered a royal path leading to Lacan since, being historical materialism, it indicated that true theoretical antihumanism and true materialism were present in Lacan. This was new since it was no longer about a Freudian Marxism within which some Leftist intellectuals tried to fit together elements taken from Marx and Freud (Marcuse, for example). The path opened up meant a renewal of Marx's texts because it proposed two returns: one to

Marx, elaborated by Althusser and far away from other humanist interpretations, and another to Freud, elaborated by Lacan.

First, I would like to highlight the pendular effect that is at stake between fantasy and ideology. I will begin by proposing that, between these two terms, we can establish a relationship of reciprocity and difference. I consider that Althusser's foundational 1970 text, "Ideology and Ideological State Apparatuses," is a key text for clarifying the matter, a theoretical base that can present itself as the condition of possibility for thinking the relationship between fantasy and ideology. There is a "turn" produced in this text, given that Althusser inaugurates an absolutely original treatment with respect to ideology. I should warn that, although we may find impasses, these "dead-end streets" open a productive space for thinking because, through them, Althusser problematizes the matter by taking it to its final consequences. In this way, we find the opportunity to situate ourselves in the heart of the complex theme, a theme that remains unclosed.

In "Ideology and Ideological State Apparatuses," Althusser begins by asking himself what a society is in order to later analyze ideology. On this, one would have to do a lengthy genealogy of the concept, going to Marx's *Economic and Philosophic Manuscripts of 1844* and *The German Ideology*, as well as chapters 2 and 3 of *Capital*, specifically everything in the section dedicated to commodity fetishism. This is because Althusser clearly explains why he considers Marx's theory of ideology to be insufficient. As is known, in the classic interpretation, ideology is a sort of veil, a construction or representation that keeps the subject from seeing reality as it really is; if this ideology were to fall, the subject would then gain access to reality. According to this humanist, Marxist reading based on the famous notion of false consciousness, once communism is achieved via the constitution of a historical subject capable of setting into motion the revolutionary process, ideology would disappear – nothing would be hidden and we would live in a transparent society where all mechanisms would be recognized. We would all be equal, and there would be no misleading representations.

However, Althusser highlights that ideology is not simply a "veil" that hides reality and, consequently, he unequivocally rejects that ideology is fundamentally a false consciousness. In this sense, he distances himself from Lukács' canonical position (and his Hegelian reading of Marx) based on the category of reification and which explains how the working class can become aware and overcome ideological alienation. On this matter, Althusser questions the presumed "human essence" on which this doctrine rests, and he adopts an antihumanist (and anti-historical) theoretical position which distances him from any proposal rooted in the core of Marxism. In fact, he defines ideology as "a 'representation' of the Imaginary Relationship of Individuals to their Real Conditions of Existence." This definition takes into account the notion of Lacan's *imaginary*. The subject does not represent ideas in the manner of the Cartesian subject or of the Kantian transcendental subject, but, rather, *imagos* or, we could say, non-reflective contents.

For Althusser, through ideology one does not come to know or cease knowing reality. Instead, subjects express the way in which they live relationships between themselves because ideology refers to the field of lived relationships and not to the gnoseological field. In this way, he distinguishes between ideology and science without playing down the importance of either one. He deduces a genuine and extraordinary theory of ideology that combines findings from Freudian and Lacanian psychoanalysis by explaining clearly a problem that underlies the subconscious. The French thinker highlights the role of the subject as the product of a structure so that, according to his reading, ideology should not be treated as a mere illusion or mirage.

In this way, he affirms that ideology is eternal like the subconscious (Althusser uses the German word *Zeitlos*, the same one that Freud uses). This is truly surprising. He clarifies further that it is eternal because there is not – nor will there ever be – a historical age without ideology, without being understood as a transcendental category of omni-historical presence. That is to say, in the same way that psychoanalysis is a historical discovery but the subconscious is eternal, so Marxism is a historical theory, but ideology is not. Ideology always exists and always intervenes. This does not mean that this or that ideological construction cannot be given a date; of course, ideological moments themselves are, indeed, historical. Althusser considers that the structural and structuring function of ideology is not historical, and in this context, he will take up the questions of school and the family. Nevertheless, historical transformations have caused the heteropatriarchal foundations on which the traditional family was based to tremble. This has meant that roles have changed and that we can now speak of a family group that takes on the task of raising children. That is to say, the family has been cut through by contingent changes insomuch as it is a historical institution. Hence the theme of relationships is fundamental when it comes to dealing with the problem of ideology.

We can now understand Althusser's intellectual boldness and the consequences of his reading of Freud and Lacan: a true turn in reading Marx. His proposal to understand ideology as eternal seemed strange, particularly for someone who, in that moment of his theoretical trajectory, was trying to reestablish materialism. This interpretation had a great impact in the Marxist world, where the majority of theorists continued to suggest ideology as a response to the correlation of forces in each historical moment and according to the proper development of social relations of production. Deliberately saying, as Althusser did, that things are not this way was a serious blow to the heart of Marxist theories: ideology is atemporal – it has been, it is, and it will be present in all historical ages, including, of course, the communist horizon. In this way, Althusser's proposal opened a new Marxist perspective that was distinct from the dominant one, according to which it was a matter of overcoming ideology in order to achieve a society free of mirages and illusions, a world where there would no longer be "false consciousness" because deceptive representations would not be necessary. Althusser has in mind not only Freud in this respect (the eternal character of ideology), but he also understands ideology as *overdetermination* (using the Freudian concept theorized in relation to the dreamwork) in articulation with the Marxist category of ultimate determination or infrastructure. This means not reducing ideology to mere superstructure as it had been analyzed by the majority of Marxist thinkers.

B) Ideology and Distortion

Parting from Althusser's developments, ideology can be understood as a structure that participates both in the reproduction of dominant relationships of social production (this is one of its aspects) as well as in the constitution of the subject. For Althusser, ideology precedes us and constitutes us as subjects, causing the relationship with the real of social relationships of production to be distorted. But this distortion does not happen in a manner that we can correct. The real is in our social relationships in a distorted way. We could say that "we are that distortion" to the extent that it constitutes us. We become subjects precisely because of that distortion since it affects the subject's relationship with itself and with other subjects. This is to say, the subject cannot have direct contact with the real of the structure that determines them. If ideology fell, then there would be no real to which the subject could accede since the real constitutes the distorting mark of ideology. In this way, ideology is nothing more than a relationship with something to which the subject will never be able to accede reflexively – a kind of impossibility or deformation that constitutes it. Psychoanalysis teaches us precisely that the subject is divided and that it always has a distorted relationship to the real. It is not that there is something distorted that can be cured or resolved, but, rather, that the relationship with the real is a distortion itself since it is the trace that the impossible real leaves in the subject's representations.

Althusser, therefore, asks himself: why does the subject have to represent reality in a distorted way? In Lacanian terms, this question could be asked in this way: how is the subject constituted so that it turns out to be impossible for them to establish a relationship with the real that would not be distorted? This is a question that Heidegger also takes up in *Being and Time*. On this matter, we should remember that, for Heidegger, *Dasein* – being there – is thrown into the world. In this way, existence – namely, the subject – since it does not have a foundation to sustain it, has a burden that is unbearable but which must be assumed. Lacan, in a similar fashion, says that when the subject arrives in the world, it does so in lack, fragmented. Moreover, the body's proprioceptive information becomes uncoordinated, leaving them in a radical helplessness that only the mirror image will unify.

Evidently, with this, Althusser understands the proper constitutive form of the ideological. And without addressing ideology negatively, he says that in it, the non-knowledge of the subject is effectively corroborated since, as was explained earlier, distortion is its sole mode of relating to reality. The subject makes use of ideology as a way to organize around the void – the real – of its own reality. Ideology implies not only the site from which I do not recognize myself but it is also the site where I *do* recognize myself to the extent that the subject is constituted from an interpellation that comes from the Other (the site that we could translate as the global field of language and the unconscious). Nevertheless, it is worth making a comment on the way Althusser defines the matter of interpellation, given that he uses the hailing or moment in which an authority figure (the police officer) intercepts us in the street to ask for identification as an example: "Hey, you there!" I must say that it seems to me to be a very naive notion of interpellation. To complicate the matter, there is a superb phrase by Lacan when he refers to the dark authority of the Other, the result being that interpellation is no longer as innocent as Althusser proposes. Judith Butler, without appealing to psychoanalysis, talks about the possible punitive and debtor character that interpellation can have, and, to return to Lacan, we know that interpellation by the Other can prepare the conditions to introduce the subject into a logic of debt and blame. In this way, interpellation turns out not to be so innocent. It could be the equivalent of Freud's sadistic superego, that punitive instance that demands pleasure from us and that always finds us guilty and in debt whatever we may do, as Lacan notes in "The Neurotic's Individual Myth," referring to the Freudian case of the "Rat Man." That interpellation places the subject in a situation of debt turns out to be illuminating in this context because if there is anything that characterizes neoliberalism, it is having exploited that instance of debt. This characteristic allows us to articulate capitalism, in its current mode, with the constitution of the subject who feels in debt by and guilty of their own situation.

C) The Mirror Stage

In my view, the problematic relation fantasy/ideology appears already in the theoretical development of the mirror state where Lacan, to make matters explicit, finds a drama. This drama is produced between the ages of six months and eighteen months, going from bodily insufficiency to the anticipation of the specular image (this is corroborated in an impactful way in the experience of children who are thrown into an experience that it is necessary to realize and that they want to anticipate). The infant, who lacks motor skills and whose proprioceptive information is absolutely disorganized, obtains the first image of themselves through their reflection in a mirror. This is a provocative idea because it challenges the modern philosophical tradition by considering that no subject constitutes itself because it does not establish a relationship in a reflexive manner. For Lacan, moreover, it is necessary to see who or what figure of the Other symbolically sanctions that image, telling the child, "Yes, that is you." The importance of the mirror stage severely complicates the question of ideology by not conceiving of itself from this perspective as a mere reflection of economic interests. What we would have to bear in mind in each subject is who or what is that Other that tells them "yes, that is you" because, according to Lacan, there begins the death toll of the destiny of each one and their true journey. In other words, according to who sanctions and says, "that is you," the subject's relationship with the real and the conditions of its existence are organized. This is what Althusser implicitly calls ideology.

D)   The Relative Autonomy of the Superstructure

The Althusserian turn ends up being decisive because, beyond affirming that ideology is eternal, he also argues that the true problem posed by Marx in *Capital* would not principally be about the mode in which we would have to form a worker from a technical point of view – namely, give them their competence so they work in a business and there become constituted as a worker – but, rather, in what way ideology is convincing workers so that they subject themselves to all of this because "they want to and they must." The problem, then, is not only how to prepare them technically but, rather, how it is organized and what system of representation allows the worker to assume, so to speak, their place in social relations in the capitalist mode of production in order to cooperate – consciously and unconsciously – in its unlimited reproduction.

On this subject, following Marx, Althusser affirms that what is important in an economic formation is its mode of reproducing itself throughout time. For this reason, the notion of ideology is very important for understanding reproduction since, as we have seen, ideology is eternal and does not belong to any concrete historical moment. Having said that, to understand the proposal's reach, Althusser himself sustains that the first thing would be to get rid of the idea of the building, using the topographical metaphor, since he already knew that Lacan had substituted Freud's metapsychology for a topology. This separates Althusser from the classic Marxist interpretation taken from Marx and Engels where infrastructure is the determinate and the superstructure is determined and sustained by the dominant ideology. For Althusser, however, it is not clear that the economic base – the infrastructure – ultimately determines the whole building, sustaining the upper floors, the superstructure. Although it has relative autonomy, I find Althusser's analysis to be distinct because he uses the term "descriptive" to refer to said structure.

Let me attempt to clarify the matter. The idea that the economic base is descriptive and not theoretical means that, even though it ultimately determines the superstructure, the infrastructure cannot entirely reach it since ideology – the system of representations, or the "upper floors of the building" – has a certain autonomy. Not only does it have relative autonomy, says Althusser, but it is the superstructure itself that can intervene in the infrastructure (here, we note a certain kinship between Althusser and Gramsci). In this way, it could be that many elements that are, in principle, assigned to the superstructure (like the juridical, religious, and artistic orders, being orders that govern social relationships) themselves intervene in the infrastructure and transform it. This leaves "the building" without a metaphysical foundation since there is, then, no base to sustain it all. And I believe that Althusser was about to expressly say so, being the good reader of Heidegger that he was.

E)   The Reproduction of State Order

Here is a crucial moment for understanding why the important thing is not simply the mode of production but also the reproduction of social relations. Althusser goes on to suggest that the state has two aspects. On the one hand, the state apparatuses that are systematically violent and function by repression (repressive state apparatuses [RSAs] like the army, the police, and the courts) in his view, do not totally guarantee the reproduction of the established order. On the other hand – and this is important – the state is also an ideological apparatus. Here, Althusser distances himself enormously from the Hobbesian tradition (the state, the Leviathan) because the reproduction of the system does not rest solely on the RSAs but also counts on powerful ideological state apparatuses (ISAs). In my view, this Althusserian conception (which is, in some respects, Gramscian) is useful because the ISAs dismantle the opposition between public and private by manifesting themselves in clubs, churches, schools, psychoanalytic societies, unions, artistic expressions, and on and on and on. In this sense, Althusser elaborates on a very heterogeneous list because, unlike the RSAs, which are more ideologically monolithic, when it comes to the ISAs, he understands that there is no immediate process of unification since these ISAs include both their own critiques and their own ideological alternatives.

There is an interesting discussion according to which, for a time, specifically during the French Revolution, religion played a definitive role, ideologically speaking. However, Althusser wonders what the most important ideological apparatus for capitalist reproduction in his era is. His answer is that the pair family/school has displaced religion, affirming that both function as the main ISAs. In this way, the theme of the subject became more relevant as a problem because he was already using certain conceptualizations taken from Lacan. Althusser very clearly warned that the child could not be withdrawn from the family or from school (whether public or private) because no one can enter the social link if they have not been marked previously by these two sites; they are the epicenter through which a highly heterogeneous set of ISAs operate. On this subject, I suggest that, in a way, the question of the subject was already present in his analysis because if he affirms that the family and the school are part of the state, and if ideology is eternal, then he would have to go well out of his way to rid himself of the subject – and I think that this would be impossible.

In sum, ideology turns out to be as important as the very mode of production to the extent that the subject not only does not represent its real conditions of existence through it but, rather, that it also fulfills a function in the unlimited reproduction of the social relations of production. It is interesting to consider what is this matter's current reach because, as I have been explaining, I understand the movement of capitalism to be circular, reproducing itself indefinitely. Faced with this power, it seems as if there is no exit. It seems that we cannot say anything about how or what comes after because we are witnessing, again and again, the different ways that the mechanisms that forever reproduce capitalism keep changing, executing, and establishing themselves. Althusser would say that ideology establishes a series of procedures that are not conscious and that allow the system – in this case, capitalism – to reproduce itself indefinitely in its social relations.

According to Althusser, ideology awaits individuals in order to constitute them as subjects. This affirmation has an obvious Lacanian imprint. Before the individual is born, ideology – the system of representations – is waiting for them in order to turn them into a subject. This is because, for Althusser, the subject is defined not as the Aristotelian rational or linguistic animal but, rather, is understood as an ideological animal since ideology is the site where the subject is constituted as such. It is curious to me that Althusser did not name the Lacanina category of the symbolic because I believe that, in reality, what he attempts to situate is that both the specular image and the symbolic Other participate in this process, a process which does not have, structurally, any other way to realize itself other than distortion. It is certainly true that, for Lacan, it is not ideology that constitutes the subject but, rather, language. We have to underline, on the other hand, that ideology constitutes subjects in a way that no longer operates solely as a mechanism of legitimation of domination – here, there is an important shift in Althusser – since it now has an ontological characterization in that it concerns the very constitution of the subject. Althussser moves away from the classic definition of ideology as a system of beliefs that naturalizes and makes invisible that which dominates and oppresses us, in order to propose that it is, rather, a structural matter.

So, the Althusserian turn implies affirming that ideology constitutes us; we were simply individuals but through ideology we become subjects. Moreover, for Althusser, since ideology is unconscious, repression also occurs. There is a repressed structure that no militancy, as intense as it may be, can suspend. No matter how informed we are about the structures that determine us, we have, and we are in, ideology. There is no outside to this ideology. Paraphrasing Heidegger, "We are thrown into ideology."

From these developments, we can maintain that ideology and subject are terms that mutually correspond to one another. In this respect, I add an idea referred to earlier about the distinction that we can establish between subjectivity and subject. Subjectivity is a historical construction, but the subject is not produced by a historical moment; it is atemporal. There was always the subject: in Greece, in Byzantium, in Modernity, and now. But subjectivity *is* produced in a historical time, being the result of powerful and contingent mechanisms of power, as Foucault has shown. For this reason, distinct subjectivities are effects caused by determined external and internal elements that inscribe subjects in their era.

F)   Objective Interest

To address the problematic relationship established between fantasy and ideology, I will focus on the theme of objective interest. How is objective interest defined and understood? And to what extent do objective interests – referred to as the place that the subject occupies in the mode of production – and their reproduction determine their ideological representations? We need to pause and consider a few things to answer these questions. On the one hand, I think that the notion of objective interest has remained trapped in a metaphysics that situates it on the side of the homeostatic, but I believe that Freud is correct to say that people are moved by something that is beyond the pleasure principle. On the other hand, it is usually taken for granted that only each subject is determined by the place it occupies in the productive apparatus or by the class to which it belongs. Already in his time, Althusser correctly realized that the subject, still identifying with the opposite of their own class interests, ultimately realizes their own narcissistic self-interest. I, therefore, propose a first approximation: the subject's objective interest is not necessarily realized in accordance with the position that they occupy in the productive apparatus. This contradicts the essentialist Marxist thesis that, as is known, supposes that the exploited defend their class interests both in relationship to its image and the ideals that regulate it. Precisely, when Althusser works on the constitution of the subject by introducing elements that are unconnected to the productive apparatus, he shows that the interests that are realized are not clear and that they are much more opaque and unconscious.

Althusser gives an account of how the subject has constituted its image, allowing us to think how the Other's interpellation that says "that is you" affects it. In that instant, the subject not only constitutes the image of itself but, rather, it also organizes – and this is key – a rejection point, a constitutive rejection through which the subject defines itself. In my view, the constitution of an identity is always achieved through rejection. On this point, Lacan affirms that "that is you" (said by the symbolic Other), and while we could add the Hobbesian affirmation that *Homo homini lupus est* (a many is a wolf to another man), this is never enough to definitively pacify the subject. However, I do not believe, at all, that the subject knows what they rejected or that it is possible to reduce it to economic interests. In fact, many subjects reject "something" that is, precisely, inside themselves and about which they do not want to know anything at all. From this perspective, I consider the widely disseminated idea that a subject supposedly votes against their own interests to be trapped in a very narrow notion of class interest. In any case, it imposes a revision of the concept of interest. In psychoanalytic terms, we have to ask the question: how would we understand an "objective" interest if it were determined by the *beyond the pleasure principle*, whether by certain narcissistic satisfactions or by a sadistic jouissance or moral masochism? When fantasy and ideology come into play as operative instances, a problematic space for thinking is opened. In my view, these instances do not overlap or merge with each other, but they do account for the issue of rejection, which is at the base of the constitution of the subject. It is, therefore, very important to analyze which of the two operative instances – fantasy or ideology – is the primordial ontological condition that makes possible this rejection, understood as a structural ontological condition but not transcendent. According to Althusser, the rejection would fall on the side of ideology, even though he does not explicitly say so in his texts. However, I understand rejection as functioning phantasmatically since, in its very constitution, it has a rejection of the real as its condition. This rejection manifests itself in diverse phenomena like racism, violence against women, or the growing hatred towards poor people. As a consequence, rejection cannot be explained only by ideology; fantasy plays an important role in its configuration.

G) Fantasy

I think it would be helpful to briefly summarize Lacan's notion of fantasy to further explain the assertions stated above. First of all, fantasy is understood as the subject's response to the way they have been thrown into the world – inconsistent and incomplete – which Lacan calls the desire of the Other. That is to say, fantasy is a response to the interpretation that the subject makes of what the Other wants. And this is because language is inhabited by the desire of the Other in such a way that the subject has no other recourse for responding to it other than by constructing a fantasy. In this way, fantasy obtains protection for the subject against the invasive and coercive pressure of the desire of the Other. Secondly, fantasy is also an "order" that allows a minimal condition of stability in the coalition produced between the 'palpitating mass' of the living being and its access to language. So, in my view, fantasy goes beyond the Althusserian interpellation by putting into play how the subject has been hoped for, desired, promoted, authorized, and rejected by the Other. As we know, there is no formula for ideology, however, psychoanalysis does have a formula for fantasy: $\$ \diamond (a)$. From there, we can sustain that the conditions for jouissance, which are truly determinant in the constitution of the fantasy, are more important than the conditions for ideology. I give primacy to fantasy because I consider that ideology, as a result, supposes a secondary relationship constructed with the latent phantasmatic material, but where factors linked to social conditions of production intervene (class provenance, different influences, etc.). In this sense, I consider fantasy to be the elementary condition, putting into play the subject's relationships with jouissance and drives. These relationships are organized by fantasy in a plot and remain constant in the life of the subject. For example, seeing and being seen, the gaze of the Other obsessively capturing the image of the subject, an inaudible voice that speaks within one's self, through its machinations, imaginary disputes with rivals that do not totally distinguish themselves with relation to the subject. These examples show a phantasmatic structure whose meaning escapes what the subject wants to express through speech.

As I have signaled, parting from the Althusserian turn, the matter that concerns us gets complicated to the extent that ideology, beyond justifying the system of domination, offers a site for the organization of any system of representations. Thus, political action, revolutionary ideas, feminism, and psychoanalysis all participate in ideology. In other words, from this perspective, ideology has a productive role to play by acting upon the very constitution of the subject. For Althusser, praxis is precisely that which could transform ideology; this "emancipatory" action would have to be oriented by a science, namely, historical materialism.

H) Alternative Ideologies

In any case, the matter is extremely problematic (Althusser was aware of this, as well) because that theory functions when it comes to explaining the guarantor role that ideology plays in domination by being in service of the capitalist system and its reproduction. However, for internal theoretical coherence, the aforementioned ideological alternatives should also be understood as ideologies, even though they may consider themselves to be transformative experiences. According to Althusser, if a praxis entails a change in the subject themself and not only in others, then one could ask: what differences are there between ideologies that are in service of domination and those that are not? On this question, Marx, as we know, argues that the ruling ideas are the ideas of the ruling class.

How can you get out of ideology? Ideologies that are generically termed (left) alternatives present themselves as something exterior, confronting the dominant order with a clear emancipatory goal that is distinct from those ideologies that contribute to the permanent reproduction of power. Alternative ideologies, in different ways, aim to combat the dominant ideology from a supposedly critical consciousness. However, in my view, this is never guaranteed because, within alternative ideologies, a fragment can reappear from within the most intimate center that works in favor of that which it was confronting, that continues reproducing, time and again, the dominant power. I highlight this aspect because the "critical" stances of these alternative ideologies seem insufficient to me when it comes to explaining a possible way out of ideology. There always exists the possibility that, within them, something reappears that will cooperate with powerful neoliberal discourses and its reproduction.

In relation to this, my hypothesis is to consider an alternative to an ideology when the Other, who is implicated in it, reveals himself as "barred" in its inconsistency. An ideology is alternative, from this Lacanian perspective, when it moves in the logic of the not-all and does not close itself in an identitarian way. Ideology, as I have already said, should not be reduced to false consciousness because ideology also occurs in alternative projects. We are thrown into ideology. Lacan describes even science as an ideology of the expulsion of the subject.

In psychoanalysis, the following question is also posed: how can you get out of fantasy? We must keep in mind that fantasy is not cancelable and neither can it be eliminated through any kind of cure since only the subject, through their phantasmatic structure, "manages," in a sense, their subjective division. Fantasy offers a certain consistency and stability, thanks to which the subject does not navigate or slide infinitely along the signifier. If there were no fantasy, there would be permanent sliding along signifiers. Having said that, how can you find a point outside fantasy? Lacan finds himself up against the same problem as Althusser in relation to ideology, and, because of this, he proposes a formula that, without implying a cut with fantasy, allows giving an account of the way that fantasy A' – that of the neurotic who psychoanalyzed themself and took the analysis to their conclusion, performing a certain anamorphosis with respect to their fantasy – is not the same as fantasy A prior to this experience. A psychoanalyst is not one who suppresses fantasy. If this were the case, then the subject would approach something like the metonymic drive that characterizes psychosis. Neither can we affirm that there exists the possibility of knowing fantasy in all of its minutiae because fantasy operates in order to achieve the very strange and heterogeneous articulation between the field of meaning and jouissance. Nevertheless, psychoanalytic schools ask the subject to give an account of their traversing of the fantasy (we are now talking about the identification of the *sinthome*, but it is the same problem for the matter at hand). It is about knowing how the subject can account for the structure that determines it and how, at the time, that structure has not completely determined it because, according to the Lacanian perspective, there is a space between the determinations that the subject has received from the Other (throughout his life) and their own choice: a gap where the subject is not exhausted by that structure and that allows a certain field of maneuvers, in which it can open a path to some logic different from the previous one, which destined them to persevere in their individual founding myth or fantasy.

As stated, the same problem is presented in Lacan as in Althusser, referring to fantasy and ideology, respectively. If ideology is in service of domination, then why does an emancipatory ideology suddenly come up? If, as has been said, ideology parts from the non-knowledge of the subject and of interpellation, the transformation from ideology A (the legitimation of domination) to ideology A' (emancipation) would have to be explained. Because of this, we must carry out not only a reading of the structure that determines us but also show that the determination is not total (the antecedent to this problem already existed in Marx's famous passage, *from in itself to for itself* to achieve self-consciousness). In the same way that fantasy is not entirely closed off, there is also a space where a different ideology can operate, one that does not legitimate power or domination. In my reading, this means that, yes, there is a gap in which the subject has the capacity to realize their act (an operation where the truth of the subject is able to find a knowledge that transforms them) and operate in another mode, even remaining within fantasy and ideology.

I)   The Epistemological Cut

In relation to this matter, Althusser appeals to his well-known epistemological cut, determined and fixed parting from *The German Ideology* and the *Theses on Feuerbach* from 1845, because it is there where, according to him, a rupture is produced in Marx – a conceptual device that inaugurates the science of history: historical materialism. This terminology, coming from Bachelard in order to deal with the so-called Mannheim paradox, refers, in this case, to the fact that there is no outside to ideology. Is there a site from which we can speak of an outside of ideology? Could I, myself, affirm that what I am writing is not ideological? According to Althusser, the epistemological rupture is the key to designating ideology's exterior. Moreover, it can only be achieved through the science of historical materialism, which would have to be founded from this new angle. In any case, it will turn out to be nearly miraculous. This epistemological cut resembles what Badiou calls the Event and

Lacan the Separation. As a consequence, we can establish a parallel between epistemological cut, Event, and Separation.

Let me make this clear. For Althusser, ideology converts the individual into a subject. Badiou thinks of a rupture that constitutes a contingent and unexpected truth in a knowledge situation; a truth referred to the transformation of the speaking animal into a subject, just like what is understood in his thought when the cut is produced in virtue of a principle of fidelity to the event, and this consideration causes him to be uninterested in ideology. Finally, in the case of Lacan, separation demands that we traverse all the paths of constitutive alienation of the subject, and, from there, when the subject is captured by the "master" signifiers, they can realize the torsion, what he calls the separation. Unlike the rupture in Althusser and the event in Badiou, for Lacan a total and definitive cut is not produced, and he calls it a new civil state of the subject.

The epistemological rupture in Althusser, the Event in Badiou, and Separation in Lacan are all figures that work precisely to show a hole in reality from which one cannot free one's self. But the possibility of being outlined in a different way does exist. There is a "structural void" in the subject and in society itself, a sort of ontological gap that blocks unification by causing antagonism to fracture the social. It is not that there exists a prior flat surface that is later cracked open, but, rather, that the previous structure is the hole around which the social is constructed. In this way, the social is an effect and is generated by antagonism, and ideology is the mode that every subject has of "imaginarily" resolving that antagonism in relation to the real. And for Lacan, the real is defined by making the sexual relation impossible. This means that there are no complementary pleasures nor drives that establish links, just like there are no complements that fuse together. The real makes sexuality something that is structurally linked to substitution. Already Marx, from his logic, described a no-relation in the movement of capital, and this supposes that there is no possible social contract that would prevent the extinction of exploitation, despite some reductionist and optimistic Marxian readings that think the real possibility of success. This is not the case for Lacan, who considers Marx himself to be the inventor of the symptom.

J)   The Border Relationship between Fantasy and Ideology

Lacan understands fantasy as absolute signification in one of his main definitions, where the impenetrable factor of all arguments is underlined. I suggest that the Marxist expression "ideological mass" is in line with this definition since it refers, we could say, to the set of ideas that someone represents (for example, a right-wing citizen is against abortion, denies the existence of climate change, looks unfavorably upon immigration, reads only certain newspapers, etc.). The ideological mass (an expression recuperated by Carlos Fernández Liria and Luis Alegre) turns out to be, in my view, equivalent to absolute signification. From this perspective,

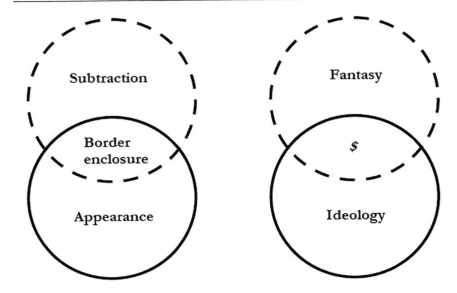

Figure 5.1 – four circles, two with dotted lines, words within

philosophers of dialogue, based on dialogical reason, are condemned to failure. In fact, people increasingly refuse to speak directly about certain matters, in this way showing the impossibility of dialogue. The ideological mass would be the peak of the crystallization of fantasy in ideology since they would shield each other and would hold impenetrable positions.

The relationship that, in my view, is established between fantasy and ideology is a border relationship, porous and spotted, where the disjunction and conjunction that occurs between the two is expressed. While it is difficult to find a structure that could articulate them, both categories resemble one another in that you cannot establish a clear exterior to either one, so there is always a relationship, through fantasy and ideology, between subject and reality. I will use a graphic, shown first by my friend Eugenio Trías in *La razón fronteriza* (*Border Reason*), to show, topologically, the relationship between ideology and fantasy, and also the site where we find the divided subject in relation to these two terms that possess, as I have already said, a family resemblance. In the figure below, I have traced a first circle where ideology situates itself (on the side of appearance), in whose area are the school, the family, and the constitution of the individual (elements described by Althusser). There is another circle with a dotted line where fantasy is found (on the side of subtraction), in which I have situated drive fixations, narcissist identifications, and the commands of the superego (elements from psychoanalysis). Finally, in the intersection, I have placed the divided subject ($), closed in by two fields: subject in the border, in the lunula where both circles surround it. The interesting thing about this graphic is that an edge of the fantasy is drawn that enters an edge of ideology, and an edge of ideology enters the area of fantasy without overlapping. And in the border area, it shows how fantasy and ideology, although different, each enter the field of the other.

Subtraction	*Fantasy*
Border enclosure	*$*
Appearance	*Ideology*

K)   Praxis

For Althusser, the notion of praxis, central to historical materialism, can traverse the threshold of ideology. How? By accessing reality? No. By overcoming the distortion of reality? No. But yes, by transforming it (reality, not Lacan's real), because we have already seen that in his proposal, the reproduction of the capitalist system constitutes the true blocking of the transformation process by not being determinant of the entire economic base. In fact, Althusser takes a good amount of time to consider Lenin's thought with respect to why the Russian Revolution happened in that country instead of others, knowing that, in Russia, none of the objective conditions described by Marx for the emergence of revolutionary processes derived from the dialectic "law" that explains the movement of social relations of production were present. On this point, Linera and Errejón had an interesting conversation (edited in Lengua de Trapo) where they propose a suggestive hypothesis, namely, that dominant classes can damage their dominant logic when they morally offend subalterns. By this, they mean when domination, instead of constituting an ordering principle and common sense which might generate confidence among the governed, sets off a moral affront to the governed. From my perspective, this thesis does not take into account Freud's thesis about moral masochism, which turns out to be very important, because capitalism has been able to exploit this superegoic instance in a new dimension. This perspective attenuates, to a degree, Linera and Errejón's hypothesis by indicating that the moral affront acts as a trigger that unleashes a collective response. There are governments that maintained power in continuous offense towards their population precisely because, in an unconscious way, the people felt deserving of this offense – a just punishment in virtue of a mythical moment of happiness that was lived in other times.

Naturally, in the sphere of the political, we must highlight the role played by both fantasy and ideology. In fact, we do not know what is going to happen or up to what point this situation where we see ever-growing societal malaise can be prolonged. Might the people consider themselves to be deserving of this or that punishment? And if it turns out that the Other does not promise better well-being but, rather, precisely the opposite, and thus people choose to keep feeling bad? In my view, fantasy *can* have a bearing on the political, in line with what Althusser affirms when he says that ideology constitutes the subject. He is indicating that this fastening or subjugation bears on social relations. On the other hand, the political does not bear on phantasmatic representations.

Society, as I said earlier, cannot be totalized because it is never closed in on itself. However, the subject lives by social ties, meaning it has its own fetishes and chooses between options (the subject does do something). Even though there is no sexual relation, in the Lacanian sense, there is love, desire, and pleasure. On this, Lévi-Strauss, in *Mythologiques* and *The Savage Mind*, points to a sort of theory of the unconscious by taking up what he calls an undecidable sequence that looks a lot like what Lacan calls fundamental fantasy. The French anthropologist discovered that, finally, behind all myths, there is a single matrix that refers to the attempt to resolve an original asymmetry or disparity. In my case, I call it a dislocation, or an antagonism. Lévi-Strauss takes the same starting point as Lacan's theory of the four discourses, but, in his case, he resolves it in mathematical terms and, in algebraic form, he explains the rules of the transformations that are produced from the founding myth. Thus, he underlines that the variations, analyzed in different historical inscriptions, originate in a single symbolic matrix that is always present in the changes. With this, Lévi-Strauss highlights that myth is not separated from *logos* as something prior, but that it responds to an impossibility that society does not resolve (the "savages" are explained within a logic, not as if they were mentally underdeveloped). Following the same criteria as Lévi-Strauss, Lacan, in the previously cited "The Neurotic's Individual Myth," also presents a series of variations on the Freudian rat man to highlight that "something" inhabits the subject – a myth that precedes it, the fantasy of each one.

Lacan's fundamental fantasy thus ends up being Lévi-Strauss's undecidable sequence, which is the way that each subject accepts the division and, therefore, that there is no sexual relation, but at the same time the subject organizes a "fix" that has a bearing on the political. In any case, the field of possible action has to do with the derived consequences; that is to say, the matter is not so much the knowing as such or the act as such, but, rather, *how* what you know is transformed. Actions have, in one way or another, an ideological and phantasmatic meaning – two large inertias that, as I have already signaled, are eternal. In other words, fantasy and ideology are not mere knowledges, but they refer to a *know-how-there* where truth and knowledge meet, but without unifying or totalizing. From a Lacanian perspective, in all of these philosophical proposals remains a materialist theory of the Act to be elaborated, a theory that would attempt, eventually, to clear up the ideological mass that, in its moment, has been able to consolidate itself in relation to fantasy and ideology. Because of all of this, I suggest that the (border) relationship of conjunction and disjunction that is established between both operations becomes the axis of the political problem.

We can illustrate the complex relationship between ideology and fantasy through an analysis of growing European nationalisms. In my view, these are not merely ideological phenomena since I understand racism and xenophobia to be structured according to the fantasy that there exists an other who could rob us of pleasure that, structurally, is always poorly distributed. From this psychoanalytic perspective, we can explain why the European feels threatened by that other who, furthermore, would not know how to make good use of that pleasure (they would waste it) and, therefore, what should be done is to reestablish a national identity that would protect Europeans from that intrusion. Obviously, this phenomenon does not occur only in Europe. This threat of the other constitutes the very nucleus of the xenophobic organizations of the ultra-right that have recently emerged in various countries. In them, there is an appeal to hatred towards the other that would "take away what is mine." The social nativism on which these ultra-rights are based may be the final form through which neoliberal mandates definitively close down social space and achieve the deadly petrification of identities by transforming them into social agents that have emerged from hate, in this way covering up their true antagonisms. If these orders – external and internal – were to achieve the plugging up of practices that journey towards that increasingly difficult and distant work of emancipation, then they would accomplish what I have, in other texts, called *capitalism's perfect crime*.

All those practices that aim to demonstrate that speaking, sexual, and mortal beings are not constituted as such on material and economic bases are, today, more relevant than ever. Both Freud and Lacan have shown, through different theoretical and clinical procedures, that the root of the subject does not belong to one's native soil, rather, identity is forged in the symbolic relation that the subject establishes with the factual site of their birth – which means that this relationship is also political. If a whole is homogenized when facing an exception that threatens it with its bizarre enjoyment, then the logic of the universal and the exception will be consummated, allocated by Lacan to the masculine logic of sexuality that "for-alls," a whole that is assured facing an exceptional exteriority that, finally, will become internal. It is the same kind of *jouissance* attributed to bad foreigners. And it is not a cultural or biological matter but, rather, strictly a logical one. In this way, the true ethico-political challenge consists of loving one's native soil without making identity into an emblem that is based on the rejection of the other.

L)   The Place of Myth

From my perspective, the above refers once again to the matter of myth in relation to the pair fantasy/ideology. On this matter, I suggest that there are two great and powerful myths: first, the myth expressed by Marx in *Capital*, called the myth of primitive accumulation, and second, the myth proposed by Freud in *Totem and Taboo*, which he calls the primitive horde. I will stay, for a moment, with Marx's myth in order to connect it with the problem of the emergence and movement of capitalism related to ideology and fantasy. It is known that Marx studied both the economists who had written before him (especially Adam Smith and David Ricardo) and Hegel's *Phenomenology of the Spirit* and the *Science of Logic* in order to give an account of the real movement of history, expressed in his theories of dialectical materialism and historical materialism where, as is known, the successive and immanent historical transformations are explained that lead to the emergence of capitalism as a mode of production. However, he is presented with a big problem when he goes back to the origin, before there was an extraction of surplus value or merchandise, because how and at what moment did the accumulation of wealth arise? Here he resorts to "mythical violence" to understand how primitive accumulation was produced, and he says that there was a group of rich people who beat poor people to death and kept everything they had. If we wanted to seek the origin of the patriarchy – which, on the other hand, implies a separate discussion – we could probably situate it in this mythical scene because in that moment of violent dispossession where some beat up others, it was women and children who suffered the gravest consequences. Having said that, there is also a liberal version of this myth derived from the British philosopher John Locke in the 17th century and continued by other British economists that is embellished in this way: on one side, there were lazy people, and on the other, there was a group of people with foresight who knew how to save and saw the future, organizing the distribution and functioning of riches because they had a project. In this myth, meritocracy became the axis of the internal logic of the production of riches, given that the "hardest working" people constitute – by their own merits – the nucleus for understanding how the accumulation of riches originated, unlike the lazy people who do not know anything and do not have projects. On this matter, Rosa Luxemburg has an interesting observation relative to this myth. She affirms that this mythical version continues in countries of the so-called Third World, in "subaltern" countries in the capitalist world, who have been incessantly and scandalously dispossessed of all their material goods, whether it be lithium, gas, or diamonds, just to name a few. The myth of primitive accumulation is therefore introduced into contemporary structures in different ways. The reserve army that Marx himself describes is nothing else than having a sector of the population unemployed so that those who are employed do not bother with demanding higher salaries and so that those who do form part of the system can consider the unemployed to be their enemies, and not those who manage the structure. We are now witnessing an interesting ideological-phantasmatic phenomenon. For example, the ultra-right has carried out a sleight of hand that situates the true enemy in the reserve army – constructed by the owners of media – and not in the owners of the media themselves (for example, Vox, the main extreme right party in Spain, a party who screams on and on about immigrants but says nothing about the Spanish stock exchange or the financial oligarchs).

M)   Human Need

To continue with the question of the pair fantasy/ideology, I now want to refer to the matter of human need, something that Marx never took up, even though both human necessity and material need appear at various points throughout *Capital*. To start, I suggest that the functioning of the capitalist system's structure does not respond to any human need – Marx obviously saw this very clearly. Yes, you can think of the human needs of the owners of the means of production as specific needs for their status – luxury, opulence, jewels, expensive suits, fancy restaurants – but these particular needs do not satisfy, in themselves, any human needs. In this regard, Marx appears to be in agreement with what Lacan calls capitalist discourse because the owners of the means of production may buy designer clothes, may purchase luxury yachts, may travel to exotic locations, etc., but they can never escape a law that is immanent to the system itself, which brings them to accumulate indefinitely. As Marx says, surprisingly, this does not mean the accumulation of pleasure but, rather, the pleasure of accumulation. This is because they do not accumulate in order to enjoy, but, rather, if there were satisfaction, it would be precisely a satisfaction of unlimited accumulation, so even if they were able to have everything, if they left behind the war of competition and were displaced from capitalism's limitlessness growth and the circular movement demanded by it, then they would be kicked out of the system. Marx warns that we should not look for a solution that would fix individualism because the capitalist subject is not moved by human need, rather, it is the structure itself that needs it. The capitalist is also subject to the rules of the system; they must enter into it no matter what – it is imposed onto them from beforehand. Marx develops this question in his discussion of fetishism to describe the logic of the structure.

I want to insist that no structure responds to a determined human need. But this opens the question: to what does it respond? For Marx, it would be about a process of unlimited accumulation because capital is defined by a circular movement without limits so that human beings have no recourse other than to maximize their value in order to yield more and more in the capitalist system. Heidegger pays a great deal of attention to what Marx says in relation to human need in spite of being anti-community, and, in the "Letter on Humanism," he says that Marx is the only author with whom he can dialogue because he sees, from a different theoretical vantage point, that he has described a gear that no longer belongs to the human condition. Although Heidegger explains, already in the 1930s, the machinery of *technē* as a mechanism that propels itself unlimitedly by transforming every being into value, he nevertheless does not conclude that the metaphysical realization of *technē* is the main effect achieved by capitalism.

The overcoming of metaphysics insistently demanded by Heidegger proceeds, in my view, from the non-relation imposed by exploitation in a similar fashion as the inevitable antagonism that this non-relation determines, and not so much by the acceptance of a repressed decision. If Heidegger had taken into account Freud's concept of repression (*Unterdrückung*), it likely would have led him to the "Jewish" question, which, as we know, he sought to avoid at all costs. The Heideggerian notions of concealment, avoiding, or forgetting express, from my point of view, a not-wanting-to-know anything about fantasy because, according to Lacan, fantasy is what is fundamentally repressed. Fantasy is constructed starting from an undecidable signifier in the first encounter with the desire of the Other into which we are thrown. Fantasy behaves like absolute meaning without being trapped by dialectics, and it permeates our ideology. In contrast, Heidegger imagined an overcoming of metaphysics via an event, a sort of step back that was lost in the madness of the confines of poetic writing, even though it was no longer about the terror of Nazism, still anchored in being. Nevertheless, that drift leaves out the only human experience that can reunite the singular of each one with the experience of the Common. I have attempted to show this in other texts in the proposal of a Lacanian left in order to give more vigor to emancipatory projects, understood as a way of sharing our solitudes. Such a thing would only be possible (a path towards emancipation, an Other left) if a decision in absolute difference were produced with the coming of a symbolic experience of the political where the "authentic equality" expressed in my syntagm *Common:Solitude* were made manifest.

Just like how, for Lacan, fantasy is not a personal experience or a result of psychological states but instead constitutes something that occurred in the subject's entry into a structure that preceded and constituted them, for Marx, the immanent logic that capital imposes is similar. No one can separate themselves from the structural pressure. This led Lacan, in capitalist discourse, not to establish a difference between owners and workers by analyzing the matter and equating surplus value with *plus de jouir*. Marx affirms, "They do not know what they are doing, but they are doing it," when he was still working on the concept of ideology. He later left this category behind when he took up the question of fetishism after seeing that the very supersensible and mystical functioning (phantasmagoric, in my terms) of the commodity does not need an ideological rupture, so that the world is doomed to function (this is what he calls the moment of formal subsumption). It seems evident that, for Marx, no one understands the remarkably complex structure of this system they live in for one fundamental reason: the capitalist system was not conceived for human needs. This is chilling – discovering in *Capital* that none of the operations realized by capitalism (for example, the selling of labor power or the structural pressure over the capitalist to pursue limitless growth) responds to human needs. As a consequence, there is no anthropology or psychology (we can leave aside the psychoanalytic question) that could properly explain why the capitalist system functions like it does. From there, we can see the theoretical antihumanism that Althusser was able to understand in Marx. The system functions autonomously and is, therefore, indifferent to human needs. A separate question is if it is indifferent to the death drive and to *plus de jouir*, given that Lacan, as I have said, establishes an equivalency between surplus value and *plus de jouir*.

Peter Sloterdijk follows this line of thinking when he suggests that cynical reason now prevails. This could be summarized in the formula, "I know how things work, but nevertheless, I do them." What does this refer to? It would no longer be "they do not know what they are doing," referring to ideology as non-knowledge or concealment. Presently, for example, it is known that there exists a reserve army made up of exploited immigrants, and it is also known that the commodity is not an object set before me but, rather, that it is an ensemble of relations: "we do it" (the army is taken to be natural or immovable). Even assuming that you know, does this mean that you can stop doing it? No. The problem of ideology is not on the side of knowledge because one can perfectly describe certain operations and, nevertheless, not be prevented from carrying them out and reproducing them. If we go to the Marxist register, supported by Lacan, we would have to see whether we put the accent on the knowing or, rather, on the doing. Sloterdijk's approach to the matter seems, to me, correct because, in the sense expounded upon here, I do believe that cynicism is realized.

I will take the opportunity to introduce here what Fukuyama has proposed with regard to cynical reason in his book *The End of History and the Last Man*, something that I think has not been dealt with sufficiently. We must remember that Fukuyama was a disciple of Kojève, one of Lacan's teachers and a great Hegelian. The end of history proposed by Fukuyama does not imply the end of ideology – even against conservative sectors that announced a post-ideological era after the fall of the Berlin Wall. Instead, it highlights the triumph of an ideology. This ideology would have hegemonically defeated communism and fascism. Precisely, Fukuyama names liberalism the dominant ideology that consists of market economies, parliamentary democracy, and the rule of law. He says that there is no alternative form of organization since every country, sooner or later, whether they aspire to it or not, will end up with liberalism. In this way, his proposal is Hegelian, given that negativity (the motor of the dialectic) becomes inoperative in the end when it has been assimilated in absolute knowledge where difference is subsumed in the final reconciliation. Fukuyama proposes – beyond his terrible intentions – that there is no alternative to liberalism (the dominant ideology) which has ultimately won the war. Unlike other theorists who, from the right, announced the end of ideology, Fukuyama highlights that this ideology has won and that there is no cut with respect to it. I would now say that reality has proven him to be right. There is no cut. If "doing" is understood from the notion of *act*, without having some exterior point as a reference, we could suggest a possible exit from the dominant and triumphant ideology, neoliberalism. We have to insist on a *know-how-there*, always contingent and conjunctural, to be able to avert that which precedes us and is imposed upon us as historical destiny. If there is no "subversive" interruption in the sense here exposed, what I call "capitalism's perfect crime" would be, once again, achieved.

Chapter 6

Exploitation

Oppression

From a new place, I want to continue thinking about the logic of neoliberal domination. In this moment, we can recognize two main aspects of this domination, aspects that, in many cases, are not cleared up in an appropriate way without two principal lines of this domination being understood. First, we find it in the classic Marxist reading that emphasizes the extraction of surplus value from the exploited classes and in the social relations of production that are perpetuated in unlimited reproduction thanks to both phantasmatic and ideological operations. In my view, however, this classic Marxist position (which is recreated in various contemporary readings) is not able to give an exhaustive account of the specific way in which the mechanisms of power oppress different classes: women, the disabled, queer people, trans people, immigrants, etc. For this reason, I think it is helpful to distinguish between exploitation and oppression. Exploitation, in Marxist terms, refers to the extraction of surplus value through insertion into the capitalist apparatus when one sells their labor power. Even though with new modes of finance, virtual, or fictitious capital it may appear that surplus value is no longer extracted, I suggest that it is never totally canceled. Nevertheless, paying attention once more to what Foucault has said, oppression would proceed in the different ways in which power relationships and its strategies occur, above all with respect to subjectivities that are set apart from dominant normative codes: immigrants of different origins, trans people, etc.

In the case of oppression, it is bodies themselves that receive the imprint in a way that is different from those bodies that are included in the exploitation of labor power. In capitalist exploitation, the body is abstracted as labor power in order to acquire value in the form of a commodity. The life of the body endures a violent and impersonal abstraction in becoming a commodity. However, as an effect of oppression, the lives of bodies are marked by fire in an immediate way, in their most intimate being.

These two aspects are inscribed in the intersection between Marx and Foucault, and specifically in neoliberalism, both aspects cross each other. Even though exploitation of labor power does not totally explain the singularity of different oppressed sectors, this does not imply that there are no operations that work on

DOI: 10.4324/9781003409410-7

their subjectivity, as we can observe in the so-called "reserve army" and that currently have found a new extension in migrant, marginal, precarious, or excluded work. As a consequence, we have to understand oppression well, taking into account its development under specific conditions of capitalism. As singular as the forces exerted over dissident sectors may be, they themselves are not entirely exempt from the regime of exploitation. Exploitation and oppression do not cover each other entirely, but neither are they totally separate. In this sense, exploitation and oppression would have a relationship of exclusive reciprocity. We could say that workers, in their own different ways, are the protagonists or the potential actors in the field of exploitation, much like women (thinking from distinct feminisms) constitute the privileged field of oppression. We should not separate oppression from exploitation like classic readings of Marxism so often do, a reading that cannot give an account of the articulation of distinct oppressed sectors in the frame of an emancipatory project, sometimes considering them irrelevant. This happens when oppressed sectors only strive to recognize their differences and deconstructed identities and maintain themselves in pure vindication of their singular existence because this can be reabsorbed in the internal movement of capital.

The "difficult left" (and therefore the "difficult emancipation") should assume that there is a relationship of conjunction and disjunction between oppression and exploitation. Since I allow myself to speak of the difficult left, the problem of the subject of the unconscious – which in its structural starting point lacks an identity to represent it – cannot be left out. In my judgment, the first right of the speaking, sexuated, and mortal being is being able to speak in a language that is not that of the exploited nor that of the oppressed. In no way does this imply canceling or dissolving the reality of exploitation or oppression. On the contrary, it is to defend a place in the subject that could not be reached by these operations. That is to say, speaking from an extraterritorial place that diagonally cuts through the identities of the exploited and the oppressed. Still, this "atopic" character of the subject of the unconscious constitutes the opening that would allow, from the logic of desire, influencing the two aspects analyzed.

Here, then, is the complete range of the difficult left when it comes to thinking about the logic of emancipation in the 21st century. If there were a possible transversability that characterized left populism in its political articulation, it would be that of assuming the challenge of finding an order of composition in the political fight, both that of exploitation and oppression. At the same time, psychoanalysis would have no reason to be the only experience where singular existence in its sexuated, speaking, and mortal condition would speak from a site irreducible to any identification, whether it be those that belong to exploitation or those that belong to oppression. But I do not dismiss the possibility that experiences inspired by psychoanalysis also attempt to sustain a locus of enunciation where a diagonal between exploitation and oppression might exist. Finally, the work of finding a way to articulate the logics of exploitation and oppression under the domain of capitalist discourse and seeing the consequences that neoliberalism implies would have to include drawing a map that concentrates on the problems of emancipation.

In short, it is a matter of separating the two aspects – exploitation and oppression – to recognize them in their specific singularities and thus inaugurate the historical project that can bring them together for the same cause.

Chapter 7

Antagonism
Conflict

Social antagonisms also traverse the conflictive practices that are organized and arranged among different movements: queer, trans, LGBTI, etc. Often, homosexual men and women remain captured by sectors of the economic elite or elite intellectuals who belong to the academy. Paradoxically, then, they are inscribed in the same world that segregates the excluded, the persecuted, and the repressed: poor queer people, workers, precarious trans men and women who are exploited by capital. Because of this, we should also distinguish between conflict and antagonism. Neoliberalism demands a confrontation that is ready to face capitalism's powers of reproduction, the power that introduces a series of tensions and conflicts in the very interior of every constellation of the aforementioned movements. In fact, we can see how, in different international media, right wing media figures who used to oppose alternative identities with heteronormativity and the patriarchy later made use of the advances made by those groups to justify, for example, xenophobia towards the Muslim world. In this way, it is common to observe in the Democratic party in the United States how they justify, in the name of "multicultural tolerance," military hostilities towards Muslim people. We can also note how many large corporations that exploit third world children come up with publicity campaigns that are favorable to these movements, and find rhetoric capable of questioning normative codes from within the logic of the market.

The conflict between multiple non-normative identities with relation to heteropatriarchal domination should never annul or erase the social antagonism that traverses them. We can still see how, in many workers' unions, there exists a great indifference with respect to these oppressed sectors from a heteropatriarchal point of view. We must think about the ways that alternatives to heteronormativism are sometimes captured by neoliberalism. The conflict between non-normative identities and heterosexual popular sectors must not be the final word on the matter, given that it is not the final reason for social antagonism. Thanks to these movements, there does not exist a unified world without fissures. It is good that this is so. In sum, there exists important conflicts that traverse these projects – projects that can cross each other and even be included, if necessary, in the constitutive antagonisms of the social. The open and interminable condition of the task of emancipation will always depend on that possible articulation.

DOI: 10.4324/9781003409410-8

Chapter 8

Promoting Hate

In our era, we are witnessing how the right and ultra-right are promoting hate because they know that the terrible Covid pandemic represents an opportunity that they will not let go to waste. It is not that these leaders have special skills or abilities, rather, they go along with what the very mechanisms of power have generated, without any particular cunning, through discourses and policies that are clearly identified with the neoliberal project. The hatred of the Other generated among specific sectors of the population slowly transforms into a rejection of the political – currently a central question – if we think of the different ways neoliberalism appears in its various forms of intervention. Lacan's well-known definition of racism, that racism is the hatred of the other's enjoyment, should be understood as a new factor in the rejection of politics.

Because of this, one of the most important questions is how to keep this hate from extending itself beyond the ultra-right. For those who have crossed that line and are already touched in their very being by the "non-political" rejection, it will be difficult to find a new anchor that might allow them to leave the delirium that has invaded a significant part of the social fabric. This has to do with a certain stupor that capitalism itself produces in human beings, where one never figures out who is really pulling the strings of the economy and politics in capitalist globalization. The conditions of possibility for the functioning of the phantasmatic/ideological neoliberal machine and its mechanisms of power demand a threatening logic. This threatening logic consists of paranoia, hatred, and accusatory suspicion moving throughout social ties and growing exponentially. This hatred is the tool through which, in the communitarian desert of capitalism, some social sectors conquer the provisional closure of their own identity by rejecting the foreigner.

The "foreigner function" can be occupied by distinct figures ranging from immigrants, women, or the oppressed of different classes, but also large international figures who are granted an unlimited power of intervention. These affective tonalities apply even to legitimate governments, even if it is progressive or national-popular, by considering it "subversive" for the nation. Lacan's thesis is therefore being fulfilled: *paranoia is personality, and the entire world is delirious.* If we add to this that the pandemic has the structure of a nightmare, the result is that subjects face each other upon waking up before the uncanny. What is new now is

DOI: 10.4324/9781003409410-9

that paranoia (in this case, a paranoia that, in many aspects, is structured differently than what is presented in the clinic of psychosis) turns out to be entirely in accordance with the neoliberal spirit. This is why I believe that the ultra-right constitutes a Plan B of neoliberalism and puts all of its ideological artillery within reach.

In our era, we can recognize the different symbolic fissures that the capitalist Other imposes on subjectivity, throwing it into the world without any of the minimal support that these symbolic coordinates make possible by being intervened upon by that Other. But neither extended depression nor the new paranoid push ever constitute symptoms for the subject in its singular experience of the unconscious (they are "unsubscribed from the unconscious"). In the absence of these coordinates that frame the world, the subject's phantasmatic reality is blurred, and the "I" libidinizes itself, giving form to an "individual" who tries, through any means possible, to extend their personality through delirium as the search for a possible justification for the helplessness into which they are thrown. They never totally achieve it.

In this regard, we have to observe the different manifestations that were produced against government-mandated health measures in different parts of the world during the pandemic. These protesters, as I have already indicated, did so in the name of freedom. From a psychoanalytic angle, we can understand how this constituted the "delirious and paranoid version" of the society of control that was outlined above. For many, it is a true insult to the Enlightenment and Marxist traditions that pandemic denial came to be associated with the "libertarian" when what that freedom cathartically demands is nothing more than their right to hate and even to take revenge. This link between freedom and hate constitutes, precisely, one of the realities that neoliberalism has been able to consolidate. In this way, the final route of these libertarian's delirium resides in the megalomaniac receptacle of the ultra-right. These "defenders of freedom" do not desire any sort of sacrifice, rather, they prefer killing over dying, imbued with hatred towards a supposed dictatorial power that they believe is restricting their rights.

Even though the current ultra-right does not have original ownership over hate, a new economy of hate has resurfaced in such a way that the paranoid allegations have entered the mental territories of the speaking beings who, even belonging to the most excluded strata of society and suffering inequality, assume that their liberty and private property are threatened by imminent danger, without knowing what it consists of. We must say that this extreme right is precisely the one that invents danger and exploits a sinister dimension in the subject. It has understood this very well since its historical function appears to have as its objective refusing truth and ethics at the margin of any public use of reason in order to execute, then, a permanent homage to the death drive. This induces a political embodiment of hate. In our era, the work that the worldwide extreme ultra-right is carrying out when they accuse progressive European and popular Latin American governments of being totalitarian is directed toward carrying out a "democratic coup d'état" in the name of freedom. We saw this in the January 6, 2021, assault on the US Capitol which looked like a carnival – like a sort of freaky sequel to Batman where many of the coup plotters were disguised (animal skins, horns, etc.) and revealed a delirious ecstasy in their faces. They were not alone since their leaders had encouraged them by sharing their goals: a fierce anticommunism and ultra-nationalist position. The majority of the assailants belonged to a poor segment of the US population – the so-called "white trash" – who, by violently taking the Capitol, showed a bizarre and conspiratorial understanding of democracy since they were appropriating it for themselves: insanity and neofascism knotted up through hate.

If this assault can still be called "populism," then the cards of liberal hope that are hiding the true face of the enemy have not been played. Europe (who watched the assault behind a scandalized gaze) secretly fears seeing in the Capital assault its own historical development. Once again, everything that the enlightened spirits think cannot happen, happens. Nothing is irreversible when the great names of the public sphere and politics have been perforated by capitalism and are now replaced by delirious constructions that no longer respond to so-called objective "interests." It is, again, about ideology in its most subjective and deadly version. As I said, an ultra-right current that emerges from the most sinister site of American society threatens with the unprecedented fact of an anti-constitutional coup d'état rehearsal. In this way, the ultra-right definitively shows that it does not accept democratic rules, despite the fact that Democratic Party will never initiate a truly transformative project, as we now see in Biden's moderate leadership. Now it is about permanent siege since a new will to power is emerging that captures an important sector of the population. This is why we attempt to decipher how what used to be called the "democratic right" appears to be on the path to extinction in our era.

In what follows, I will indicate a few characteristics of its unfolding:

1. The ultra-right has lost its inhibitions and is now shameless. They ask themselves again and again, what authority do democratic governments have to make us remain in our homes? To achieve the mobilization of many layers of society, the ultra-right count on an uninterrupted depoliticization of large sectors of the population that started in the 1980s and that was re-signified during the pandemic, out of the new atmospheres generated when life is conceived only in terms of survival.
2. When a democratic and sovereign government attempts to be progressive, a media mechanism that functions at full capacity in favor of the right is set off. This operation no longer needs a classic coup d'état; a gradual and sustained tendency that perforates democracy in any way possible and even advances toward a state of exception is enough. We must recognize the effectiveness of this step, above all when, in a powerful way, the connection between the apparatuses of the media, social networks, and judicial power is established. The right's traditional xenophobia and racism have slowly spun towards this much more effective position that sustains them where, as I said before, they end up calling "foreign" any government that does not respond to their interests.
3. The ultra-right now knows, even if only tacitly, that its current mission consists of keeping transformative projects from continuing, and they have concluded

this implicitly, without the need to explain it in any global congress. This power claims to situate itself above international organizations, which, in turn, are treated as useless appearances.

4. The worldwide ultra-right has, more than ever, casual and accidental representatives. Their names do not matter much since they are mere transmission belts of neoliberal dictatorship. For example, the social current that led to the presidency of Donald Trump can continue to sediment itself in the social fabric even though he lost the 2020 election. This is what is dangerous.

Moreover, the dialectic between opposition and government in the places where a progressive or a leftist national-popular government exists is breaking down day by day. Without going into philosophical subtleties, the dialectic always implied a minimal recognition between adversaries against a superior instance that, even if it did not cancel antagonisms, did regulate them under the idea of democracy. The pandemic and economic disaster that accompanied it led the ultra-right to the deterioration of this dialectic.

In online networks, media apparatuses, and international financial systems, it appears to have been decided that treating democratic and progressive governments as communist, dictatorial, and anomalous aberrations is appropriate. In this way, they made use of the pandemic quarantines to designate them as caprices of a communist or totalitarian dictatorship. In the pandemic, the ultra-right sees its historical opportunity to destroy the true democratic order that was won in elections, which makes them hope for the failure of the quarantines, of the ethics of care, exhibiting, sometimes, a dark and obscene satisfaction with death.

Current governments are appealing, again and again, to our personal responsibility to care for ourselves and others – good sense and prudence require that we impose self-discipline upon ourselves. The thing is that there are three problems that democratic governments cannot address since, at least for now, it is structurally impossible for them to confront them. The first, already signaled by Kant, refers to the fact that the subject's sensibility is always attracted by its particular interests, and because of this, it is easily distracted from the imperatives of practical reason. The second, based on Freud's lucid observation, has to do with the fact that modern civilizations are advancing, moved by a pressure that is increasingly stronger than the death drive. We observe the existence of thousands of subjects that do not believe in the public pronouncements of the State. It is not that they are deniers, but deep down, they think that it does not apply to them; in a way that borders on magical thinking, they feel immunized (even though they cannot figure it out). Finally, the third inevitable problem is constituted by the very conditions of capitalism, which demand living in an absolute present without the possibility of future historical perspectives – hence the apocalyptic atmosphere of our age. These problems demand that we ask a question: can leftist and popular democratic governments construct a new type of non-repressive authority that is sufficiently firm in order to give new consistency to the exercise of sovereignty? An authority where the appeal to so-called self-discipline does not constitute the final word in the pandemic?

On this horizon, everything becomes problematic, eventful, and difficult to sustain for a progressive government because the two options presented to them are complicated to implement. The first entails radicalizing itself, following the demands of the left that supports them – that is, redoubling the bet and facing the extreme right as the enemy that it is. The problem with this option is isolation and international harassment since the finance world can impose economic conditions so severe that they bring the country to a situation of impoverishment with no possibility of social improvement. The second option is sadder (pragmatic, others would say) since it entails ceding on key questions with the naive expectation of negotiating with an enemy that does not practice opposition but, rather, a delegitimizing war against elected governments because the extreme right, not having to spend its energy on governance, can devote themselves entirely to neoliberal conspiracy. In this situation, there is no leftist, progressive, or national-popular government that is not always under siege by vanishing points, incoherence, etc. These circumstances demonstrate that the State, in principle, belongs to the market, even though it will be a matter of not ceding the totality of itself to capital, transforming it into a place of dispute and war of positions so that neoliberalism will not win the entire battle.

During the pandemic, we have seen how the ultra-right has used all the means at its disposal to destroy truth in its internal structure because in the circular and unlimited movement of capitalism, it appears that no longer is anything impossible, and everything can be said. In this way, the different communication flows that circulate incessantly on social networks offer a social landscape where any message can be repeated again and again until it breaks, in the experience of the singular being, their relationship with truth. The problem is that they aim to eliminate, through various media mechanisms, any difference between a true statement and a fallacious statement. This characteristic of capitalism is not only to generate falsities but also to abolish in each subject the experience of truth by disseminating supposedly transparent information so that subjects naturalize the manipulation. This constant communication is always realized with the conscious or unconscious complicity of the subject, who voluntarily propagates and disseminates it. The excuse for carrying out this neoliberal operation is perversely realized in the name of liberty because, in this way, one can "freely" say anything in the innumerable forums available for this goal. This is how truth begins to dissolve. The processes of the concentration of capital and its different logics of accumulation are imitated with the information that is distributed, like an expansive wave, in the social fabric, carried out by the ultra-right. In fact, all over the world, we see media actors who behave in an identical fashion to that expressed by the processes of viralization. In just one day, they can say one thing and its opposite, as long as what is said obeys the imperatives of online circulation. The paradox is that, in order for a similar situation to be installed, it has required that neoliberalism unify the field of meaning around the term "liberty" to be understood as a private initiative. In this way, any activity that opposes this capture of "free" subjectivity is considered totalitarian.

Three ideologues, among others, promoted a theoretical framework sufficient for this operation to become an effective reality: Hayek, who saw in Keynes a sort of Hitler; Popper, who took science as the sole paradigm capable of orienting free and democratic society; and Fukuyama, who signaled capitalism as the insurmountable end of history. These three intellectuals decisively contributed to liberty becoming the nucleus of the meaning of the market, transforming it into a great network that searches within historical facts with the goal of integrating them into its movement. Neoliberalism is capitalism's chance to, first, demote any rupture event in order to then consider it a "novelty," in this way making the subject a participant in one of the market's key elements. The role of those agents of the extreme right is that the truth disappears. As I have explained in other texts, the truth, by definition, must be egalitarian, not subject to any hierarchy, and therefore not subjected to any power. I am referring to singular truth, where a space of a "solitary and egalitarian commons" could occur. In this aspect, I consider that facing fake news and the distinct media messages that circulate around the web, disseminated without end, there is always a remainder in the subject where the truth has a possible place to emerge.

What resources does the subject have in order not to remain trapped in the media flow network? What elements of its very constitution, from the moment the subject enters the world, can never be entirely captured by power structures? As an answer to these questions, I will say that the sequence mourning-memory-desire constitutes, in my view, the site of inappropriable subtraction for these flows that destroy truth. This triad plays in a historical temporality that is radically different from that of the absolute present that neoliberalism aims to impose.

Truth, as we all know, is a theme that has a long and fecund historico-philosophical tradition and has been theorized by two authors to whom I often return: namely, Heidegger and Lacan. Truth, in the Heideggerian sense, implies an un-concealment that, in its opening, always maintains the original concealment of the truth. In this sense, truth is a manifestation that allows what is hidden to appear, but without completely revealing itself since the essence of truth also precisely says that which cannot come to light or be said entirely. Both *non-knowing* in Heidegger and *half-saying* in Lacan express the impossibility of transparency that neoliberal mechanisms try to impose as a simulacrum of truth. There is no truth 1) without the retroactive reading of our coming into the world without foundation, 2) without the decipherment of our legacy, never fully translated, 3) without mourning the trauma that constituted us against a real that is impossible to symbolize, 4) without memory that works with the frames of that mourning where our finitude is also at stake and, finally, 5) without the unyielding insistence of desire that can house us. All of that is being subtracted from subjectivity, summoned in this way to exist in an absolute present – without history – by neoliberal operations. Once capitalism's capacity to destroy the emergence of the truth is presented, we must continue to insist – as I have been arguing in other texts – that the crime is not yet perfect. The density that capitalism increasingly achieves refers simultaneously to the homogenization and the fragmentation of reality, and that its accelerated circular movement makes it an obstacle to the truth of singular being. This perspective could give rise to understanding all of this in pessimistic terms, where impenetrable capitalism without fissures is described. Nevertheless, here capitalism finds its possible weakness. Perhaps, from one day to another, an incalculable contingency, originating from an almost microscopic view of the device's operation, can take the form of a political experience capable of derailing. Because by presenting it as a full power, paradoxically, capitalism cannot measure the symptomatic and contingent manner in which the impossible can affect its appearance, in a sort of Achilles heel that constitutes its authentic limit for its ability to capture reality. But some authors, from different perspectives, advocate for "the destruction of the system" and, as a consequence, repudiate partial transformations that can be realized from within capitalism. In this sense, they imagine the recuperation of a new power in human experience that is capable of separating itself from the capture caused by neoliberalism to treat impotence in the face of capitalism, that which makes attempts to transform it vain. However, in my view, the decisive point for addressing the place where capitalism is susceptible to creak in its foundations would consist in working with those aspects that circularity can never totally absorb. I am referring to the aforementioned triad mourning-memory-desire, since through these terms, although impossibility circulates, impossibility itself can be transitorily suspended and make political contingencies of a new sort emerge. It is not about demanding the impossible but about knowing what to do with the impossible.

Chapter 9

Popular Responsibility

What type of alliances should a left or national-popular progressive project make in order not to fall under the siege of the right? And what ethico-political substance should sustain them? The revolutionary hypothesis being discarded (which nowadays would enter into a sacrificial logic), is now the left(s) which, with limited symbolic resources, must assume the emancipatory legacies of different signs and reinvent them even if it means running the risk that, through neoliberal mechanisms, their proposals may appear to be arbitrary impositions. In every sovereign left project, an irreducible ethical dimension relative to justice underlies it. And where there is ethics, there is always a duty to renounce narcissistic drives, the same drives that the neoliberal order constantly propels.

If capitalism's power is analyzed and described in its unlimited reproduction and with its new goal of governing souls, we can understand, then, that neoliberalism constitutes a serious anthropological alteration by converting the human being into *Homo economicus*. Because of this, the question of the transformative conditions of politics becomes simultaneously decisive and cut through by serious uncertainties. We must keep in mind that capitalism has transformed itself into a giant machine capable of generating constructions that are mere mirages, having no relationship with truth or ethics. As I have already mentioned, the ultra-right is uninhibited and transgressive in its discourse and its acts, crossing any and all limits. For the left, on the other hand, it is not acceptable to say just anything or lie all the time. Political responsibility is, therefore, the business of all of those – all of *us* – who continue to insist.

Because of this, we have an ethico-political obligation to put a stop to the incessant loss of the categories that allowed for a certain intelligibility of reality beyond critiques of governments that come and go. Even though we talk on and on and analyze manipulation in social media and media blackmail using different theories, this does not absolve us of what we could call our "popular responsibility." Just like we should not blame the victims of social media manipulation or those who are on the receiving end of systemic violence that emerges from the alliance between media powers and the anti-democratic right, neither should we avoid the responsibility of singular existence in its political adhesions. It is high time that the

DOI: 10.4324/9781003409410-10

political left debated this responsibility and took into consideration the problematic matter of its articulation.

If there is anything new that Covid-19 introduced into political life, it is that there cannot be a transformative project if it does not start with an "intimate" interrogation of the desire of the community that inhabits us. In the solitude engendered by capitalism, there is no place for what I have been calling *Common:Solitude* (*Soledad:Común*), which implies that what is truly common is not the homogeneity of the masses nor the equivalential character of the commodity since *Common:Solitude* puts into play the most radical singularity of the subject as the true material support that we have and which is available to us in the commons of *language*. This *Common:Solitude*, presupposed by any collective transformative project, radically distinguishes itself from autistic loneliness promoted by capitalism. At the same time, *Common:Solitude* is the original link that can be established between the singularity of the subject and the collective and common dimension of *language*. This is the matrix that orders the relationship between the singular and the collective, and therefore the problematic notion of what is called the "historical subject" must always keep in mind that initial matrix. If it did not proceed this way, the so-called historical subject would again fall into the metaphysical network that, in different historical versions, the left has attributed to it.

At this crucial point, I must say that the well-known reasons for manipulation are not enough to explain the problems of the emergence of a popular will of the left, and we would have to go deeper into the problem of the subject and its difference with subjectivity. Because continually insisting on the matter of (supposed) manipulated consciousness implicitly obscures a surrender: establishing that, sooner or later, we will all be puppets of an omnipresent power. Just like historical religions began with the singular giving of each existence until inventing their own symbolic conveyor belts, contemporary politics would have to be able to show and deploy that which insists on each subject as that which cannot be manipulated by any system, a kind of "remainder" that names the being of the subject beyond all determination.

The "battle for meaning" and the "cultural battle," while they remain valid, are sustained by narratives whose anchor points are continuously eroding. In such a situation, the growing problem is that the representatives of neoliberal power are no longer interested in sustaining this or that program of meaning or culture – their final goal does not need them. Its narrative is inspired by contradiction and anticulture because its main pragmatic purpose is to depoliticize the population by adding different subjective crowds constituted in non-belief to direct subjects to the rejection of the political. A clear example of this is the celebrated syntagm "patriarchal capitalism" that is so frequently mentioned in our own emancipatory political project. Without a doubt, capitalism is contemporaneous with heteropatriarchal oppression, but this does not mean that it cannot continue to exist without it. Without questioning everything that faces that oppression and which carries out its eventual destitution, capitalist exploitation would not be definitively exhausted. As a last resort – and this is the main problem – capitalism is a headless machine that can reproduce itself in different historical scenarios.

On the other hand, we have started to glimpse the way in which the world vaccine market is unfolding by promoting a framework of containment determined by their therapeutic character. But, at the same time, this market is burdened by an order of geopolitical rivalry whose consequences cannot yet be accounted for. We can already see that neoliberalism is sharpening its expansion by using laboratories as means and lobbying groups over governments. As a consequence, in this panorama, neither the health gap nor heightened inequality will be closed. This is because emancipation, as I have written in other texts, is only generated if it is able to constitute what in Marxist terms is known as a historical subject (a problematic expression that, in my view, has the aforementioned formula *Common:Solitude* as an antecedent, if it is intended not as a resource that would guarantee an emancipatory project by already established principles). In order for this political construction to take place, there must be a convergence between distinct social sectors, a process of articulation and recreation of popular forces so that an antagonistic border can emerge. It is no longer possible for capitalism, from a dialectical and self-reflexive movement in its internal progression, to become aware of its destructive potential and generate a limit to its own expansion.

Many European authors, in various ways, have come up with a proposed way to exit capitalism via the so-called Bartleby effect and the phrase immortalized in Melville's famous story: "I would prefer not to." What these intellectuals have in common, more or less, is the thinking that subtraction is a condition of emancipation – in other words, a non-participation in state politics. Their various positions suggest that the state is a key part of capitalism's mechanisms, so they analyze it as theater or spectacle, where official institutions and its opposition are mere actors and where the people participate as consumers of the administration of different representations. In this sense, they promote a return to transversal experience without any link to the politics of the state.

My main objection to these proposals is that they appear to conceive of the state as something compact and full that lacks fissures. This stops them from thinking about the central problem of transformative politics. In this way, they forget that contingent and unpredictable events can occur, which, even if they do not emanate from the state, can cut through it. Because of this, I suggest that their proposals – even though they carry out a productive reading of capitalist future – converge on a sort of new, extraterritorial anarchism by making the state converge with its administrative and bureaucratic drift. While I concur with them in many aspects of their theorizations of capitalism, none appear to take into account the determining role of the superego in the subjective structure that neoliberalism produces.

Chapter 10

Blueprints of the Inappropriable

One might note a certain anthropological pessimism from the versions presented here on the relationship between capitalist discourse and neoliberalism since capitalism is here presented as a device that turns out to be unapproachable in its incessant unfolding. Nevertheless, as I have often insisted in other texts, I reject the possibility of the perfect crime. It is one thing to understand that crime as a threat and another to surrender to that which is presented to us as inappropriable by capitalist discourse. In what follows, I will speculate on certain writings of the "inappropriable," taking inspiration from a topological figure – the Borromean knot – that acquired special relevance in Lacan's later seminars. Here I distance myself from the way Lacan used this figure since I am simply interested in appropriating those aspects of it that I consider to be pertinent to my argument.

The knot is constituted by three rings that are tied together in such a way that if one of them were to become untied, the other two would also be undone. At the same time, this figure is never secured by a knotting that sustains or holds all three together. The knot, therefore, requires the presence of a fourth element to maintain the knotting of the three rings. The crossing of these knots shows an enclosure within them that is irreducible to a fixed point in the Euclidean plane. Even if we pulled each of the rings, we would never obtain a center point in the geometric plane because an irreducible void would always remain. The rings do not cut through each other – a superposition occurs, but not an intersection. In the following graphics, I will show their application between the previously mentioned terms mourning, memory, and desire:

DOI: 10.4324/9781003409410-11

Superposition ≠ intersection

Figure 10.1 – Borromean rings, blue, green, and red
Superposition ≠ Intersection

Non-relation: Irreducible void

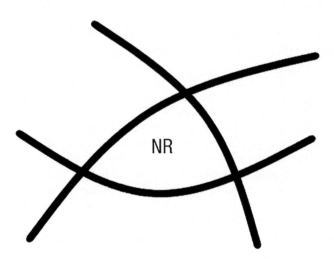

Figure 10.2 – three rings, the center of the Borromean knot with text "NR" in the center

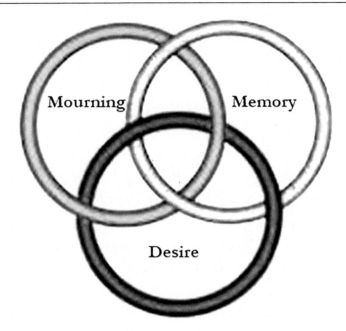

Figure 10.3 – Borromean knot with "Mourning" "Memory" and "Desire" in the rings

As we can see, there is no intersection, but there is a superposition of mourning, memory, and desire which establishes an enclosure with respect to the nonrelation. This shows that impossibility emerges since there is no move from one term to another. This expresses the superposition of the rings, which should be differentiated from their intersection. In other words, precisely, that irreducible void is always the site of a non-relation that shows that the three knotted terms are traversed by a constitutive impossibility between them. We should recall that Lacan situates the sexual non-relation as a void that is impossible to fill in the very heart of collective life. For Lacan, the sexual non-relation implies an impossible real, given that there is no mathematical formula that could establish a relationship of proportion between the different forms of enjoyment, whatever the genders or sexes may be. The speaking, sexuated, and mortal being (however they identify or whatever form of enjoyment they practice) would never be exempt from this impossibility and so must replace it with different, supplementary resources: phantasms or *sinthomes*. "Sinthome" is not about a pathological or morbid symptom but, rather, the invention of singular existences facing the real impossibility of the sexual relation.

The triad mourning-memory-desire is inappropriable for the demands of capitalist output that push all human experiences towards an absolute presence. The

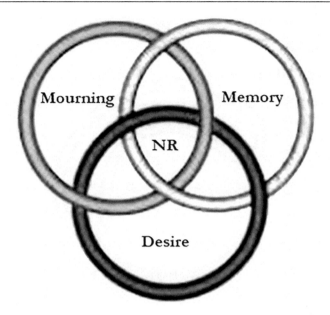

Figure 10.4 – Borromean knot with "Mourning" "Memory" and "Desire" in the rings, "NR" in the center

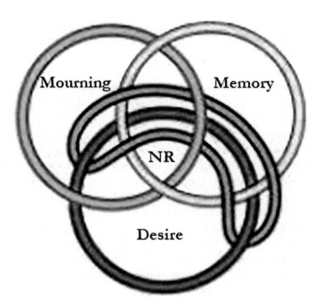

Figure 10.5 – Borromean knot with fourth 'ring', "Mourning" "Memory" "Desire" and "NR"

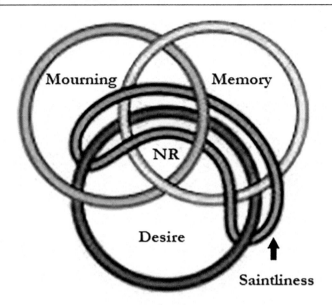

Figure 10.6 – Borromean knot with fourth 'ring', "Mourning" "Memory" "Desire" "NR" and "Saintliness"

non-relation in the central void is what makes the knotting between these three elements effective.

By mourning, I mean an active experience; it is not nostalgia or melancholy for something lost. It is a task that requires elaboration with everything that concerns our historical legacy and our symbolic inheritances in both the singular and collective dimensions.

In Seminar X on anxiety, Lacan argues that we only mourn for that or for those for whom we have been their lack. But, as is often the case with Lacan, we must be careful with this expression. In this case, "their lack" does not mean that we would be that which would have made complete what the other was missing, but, rather, that we have occupied the enigmatic site of lack. Lack is what, initially, both the subject and the Other share because both are barred by the non-relation from the moment the subject enters signification. To mourn with respect to those for whom we have been their lack does not mean that we would complete them with our presence, but, rather, that we become responsible for the site of lack that was in those experiences or those subjects. In this way, mourning is understood as an experience of love (in both senses that Lacan gives the word love: "love is giving what you do not have to someone who does not want it" and that which "allows *jouissance* to condescend to desire." In the work of mourning, we give what we do not have since we cannot satisfy that lack. In any case, the work consists in situating oneself in that very place where we do not know what the lack that we are mourning refers to nor what we have to offer; we can only let ourselves be traversed by it. At the same time, that act of love keeps jouissance from coming back over itself. Therefore, there is an opening towards the cause of desire that comes to function as the outcome of the lack that mourning put into play.

By memory, I do not refer to the recuperation of the past nor a return to it. It occurs in a mode that is opposed to the absolute present that neoliberalism attempts to impose, in Lacan's formulation, that is presented as a double temporal movement: *what I will have been for what I am in the process of becoming.*

Neither in mourning nor in memory does an essence exist that should be recuperated since both experiences superimpose themselves in order to make a place for the space of desire, which drags them towards an indestructible insistence: the central void.

We must remember that these three rings can become unknotted, and in order for the triad mourning-memory-desire to sustain itself, a fourth ring that keeps them together is necessary.

As we can see in the previous image, I have introduced the term "saintliness." Just like what occurs in the knotting between mourning, memory, and desire, saintliness also consists of an operation that has no prior antecedent since it emerges from the very superposition of those three. Lacan privileged the figure of the saint as he who would be in the position of finding a possible exit to capitalist discourse. Lacan did not make clear why he chose that word; enigmatically, he affirmed that the saint's business is "trashitas" (*il decharite*). This expression can refer to the fact that, in this case, the saint does not distribute objects that satisfy need, rather, it operates as a cause of desire. Lacan radicalizes that formula by saying that it is "waste" which operates as a cause of desire. This waste should never be conceived of as slag. I insist that this saintliness is atheological and secular because it is constituted by the emanations from the people where mourning-memory-desire become knotted. I have chosen the word "saintliness" in order to separate it from any possible gender assignment (neither the masculine *santo* nor the feminine *santa*). I do not use the term saint (*santo*) because saintliness can inhabit more than one or the other, even the collective. There can be saintliness in everything that knots up mourning-memory-desire or, said in another way, saintliness can reach a popular movement, a leader, an insurrection, or what Lacan called *the only men of truth we have left*: the revolutionary agitator, the writer who marks language or who renews the thinking of being. Saintliness: a term never preceded by an article so that it cannot be understood as a substance or anything permanent, but, rather, a term that is about a limit that is crossed – an emergent that eventually takes charge of the unresolvable tensions between mourning-memory-desire.

This secular saintliness could indicate the path of a new militancy, a militancy that takes up what is inappropriable for capitalist discourse. If capitalist discourse exploits insatiability – that which never ceases for speakers in order to lead them to a production of themselves where any experience of the void is rejected – the saint is the figure (or the figures) that opens the possibility of separating the subjects from those deadly circuits, restoring the openness to desire. Both singular and collective at the same time since saintliness inhabits the *Common:Solitude*, saintliness is that which invents a place outside of goods and is not defined by them. That is its waste or remainder condition that, unlike slag, could be the cause of a new desire. For in true saintliness, the erotic substance of the drive must be present, unlike the obsessive ascetic. Therefore, desire in saintliness diagonally crosses the demands and unsatisfied claims directed at the big Other and that, as such, continues to speak in the language of the Other. In this respect, saintliness is also speaking and sometimes inventing a language that is not codified by the Other, open to the relationship with surplus enjoyment opening to a destiny that is different from the connection of objects with capitalist enjoyment.

In many cases, when they are perceived as Eurocentric categories, the figures of saintliness are confused with idolatry. Finally, saintliness maintains the knot between mourning-memory-desire without any of the terms imposing itself hierarchically over the other three, without destroying the knot, and without intersections that are unaware of the constitutive impossibility of the non-relation.

Chapter 11

Community, Society, State

I also propose to tie together three additional terms: community, society, and state. Between community, society, and state, there is always an underlying and central void that none of the three can fulfill. This void is precisely that which makes possible those operations that move from community to society and from society to the state. In order for the three parts of this knot not to tend towards dispersion, a fourth term that sustains the knot will always be necessary. This fourth term could be called the people-sinthome. Here, the people do not allude to a predetermined entity, something that was already there, waiting to be produced. Rather, with this expression, I refer to the historically constituted emergence in the operation of knotting. By sinthome we should not understand any type of pathology because with this term, I mean an invention that would allow for the people-event, or in other words, the creation of a political will that would maintain the knot between community-society-state. In this political will, each term intervenes simultaneously from its respective positions, and each position is included in the collective swarm of the commons.

Bearing this in mind, the subtraction of capitalist exploitation and oppression from concomitant power would not be resolved with the exodus of particular communities in whose praxis the traces of capital would be absent. A historical example of this is the Mothers, Grandmothers and Children of the Plaza de Mayo who face the crimes against humanity committed by Argentina's military dictatorship. In their spontaneous mobilization, the community was the site of emergence. Later, these fights were assumed by human rights groups belonging to society. Finally, their mobilizations were recognized by state policy. All of this was traversed by tensions, marches, and counter-marches of various types. Finally, however, the movement of the mothers achieved the knotting of these three terms and the emergence of a people-sinthome that would appropriate this contingent project of knotting. This resulted in human rights not being considered identical to themselves and not constituting themselves as a subsystem to reality. In this sense, the invention of the people-sinthome substitution led to a new way of sustaining said historical reality.

DOI: 10.4324/9781003409410-12

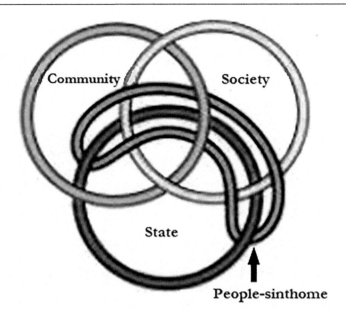

Figure 11.1 – Borromean knot with fourth 'ring', "Community" "Society" "State" and "People-Sinthome"

Both knots – the one corresponding to mourning-memory-desire and the one that refers to community-society-state – are in permanent dialectical tension, torn open on many occasions. Nevertheless, they constitute the structural matrix that, again and again, relaunches every social dynamic toward what is to come.

Chapter 12

Retroactivity

Continuity and Discontinuity

Ever since I began writing on left Lacanianism, I have insisted on Freud and Lacan's "bad news" with respect to the teleological progress that was so central to different readings of Marxism in the 20th century and that guaranteed a revolutionary destiny – communism – for the history of man. On this point, the Freudian discovery and Lacan's teachings weigh heavily on the human condition and can therefore acquire the form of an enlightened pessimism. My goal up to now has been to make use of the bad news and transform them into a new jumping-off point for the logics of emancipation, but without ignoring the fact that the anthropological pessimism of Freud and Lacan may have been accentuated, today more than ever, by neoliberal capital's incessant power. I have attempted to extend the field of the logics of emancipation to the 21st century instead of taking the matter to an "ironic relativism" or even to a "cynicism" because I believe Freud and Lacan's bad news with respect to the mirages of modern progress can serve for elaborating and constructing a project of emancipation without the metaphysical alibi of the tomorrows that herald a new day. In my view, in the 21st century, emancipation drags along with it the various implicit problems in the singular constitution of the speaking, sexuated, and mortal being –emancipation that would participate in an Enlightenment tore up by its antagonisms, popular, democratic and of the left, whose ultimate aspiration would reside in the difficult articulation between the exploited and the oppressed with its new obligation and responsibility.

Retroactivity is the condition of possibility for a historical legacy to operate, but it needs anchor points that relate to the traces of memory. The future can only be thought retroactively, not as a plan thought up in advance. If it is true that the revolutions of the 20th century should constitute a legacy that continues to interpellate us, that does not mean that memory should become an impotent nostalgia since that would lead to taking historical experiences as models simply to be imitated. Rather, it would be about making possible a path, with its faults and impasses, where political invention should translate institutionally because there are no lineal or evolutionary projects.

In the face of the Covid-19 pandemic, while at the beginning it seemed to give strength to the ultra-right, we now get the impression that the current disaster is so tremendous in every plane that I would venture to say that neoliberal discourse,

DOI: 10.4324/9781003409410-13

based on the elimination of every difference, will have a major obstacle, precisely because of the irradiation of pain that the global disease has caused and is causing. The ultra-right may not be able to continue insisting so strongly on rejection, on hatred, and on the promotion of social violence in order to orient itself towards other strategies.

Up until now, classic rights had been won by the extension of the rejection of the politics proper to the discourse of the extreme right, but now neoliberal domination doubts whether that is the best path in defense of capitalist interests. Neoliberal theorists now see that the religion of the market cannot be sustained mainly by hatred and that they must find new and more seductive forms for their faithful consumers. However, at the moment, they cannot because they fear (as always) the rise of democratic and progressive forces, who fortunately seem to be making a comeback. Perhaps we are approaching the day in which it becomes clear that neoliberalism has no mechanism that would allow it to sustain civilization.

Chapter 13

New Challenges

The ideas presented in previous chapters imply new challenges in the era of the Covid-19 pandemic. These challenges are related to political action but are also of interest to psychoanalysts since they take up the question of the subject.

The stage where the problem of a conjunction of both psychoanalysis and politics and subject and praxis presents itself turns out to be enormously complex. Long ago, the problem was formulated like this: on the one hand would be the collective, the *for all*, the field that would be taken up by politics and in which ideology (which, according to Althusser, has an eternal character) would be the form through which the state of things would reproduce themselves as a system of representations. On the other hand would be the psychoanalytic clinic which would treat the singular subject one by one, where fantasy and opaque *jouissance* would be, to the subject, proper, unrepeatable, and untransferable. In this way, it appears at first to be impossible to synthesize or find a way to join the irreducible singular (the *sinthome*) with the plural or collective (based on universalization). However, my theoretical wager deals precisely with giving a possible way out of this dilemma, a wager I have formulated and developed with the expression *Common:Solitude*, developed further in other books.

Capitalism's discourse is a sort of social tie, precisely from the moment when Lacan suggests it as a discourse – bizarre and counter-discursive, we could say, but the most important core of capitalist discourse that would need to be written with his mathemes. This is because the social link is broken. On the one hand, is solipsistic *jouissance*, and on the other hand, the universal. This is due to the fact that capitalist discourse has managed to connect the subject with *jouissance* in such a way that the solipsism of *jouissance* has become socially embodied. In addition to not being prohibited in the field of the social, it is being pushed toward the configuration of new social ties. That is to say, through the *jouissance* of individuals, capitalist discourse becomes a permanent generator of pseudo-social ties. Because of this, for many years now, I have been proposing that where there is misery, there is also *jouissance*. Capitalist discourse has an uncanny character; it manages to transform surplus value into surplus enjoyment by leading subjects to relate, as Lacan himself would say, outside of love. So a type of *jouissance* is generated in the subject that makes him feel constantly exalted because it is promised to him

DOI: 10.4324/9781003409410-14

that his lack will be fulfilled if he consumes everything that the market is offering him without respite. Even the poorest are captured by consumption, so the market is generating a simulation of self-sufficiency that continually relaunches them due to the insatiable character of the desire.

We should clarify that, according to Lacan, the articulation of capitalist discourse was not the result of the wills of corporations or of states. For Lacan, rather, the catastrophe burst into the discourse of the master after a certain relationship with impossibility was transformed, which referred to what cannot be entirely appropriated (shown in the graphic of the blueprints of the inappropriable) and that had been trapped by the conjunction between *techné* and market. From that moment, the discourse of the master could not sustain itself in its place. On this point, it is worth remembering that, for Heidegger, the entire history of the West inevitably led to the forgetting of Being. *Techné* supposes the culmination of philosophy by not occurring outside of it. In other words, both for Lacan and for Heidegger, the catastrophic transformation is produced in the interior, whether it be within the discourse of the master or the history of philosophy. As a consequence, a series of discourses appear now to have collapsed and operatively annulled because certain constitutional limits of modernity (enlightened mythologies and transformative narratives) have been suspended with no way of knowing if they can ever be reestablished. In this way, the difficult task would be to see if those symbolic legacies can still be operative against the power apparatus.

On this point, critics of Laclau often present him as a thinker who, with his autonomy of the political, extols a loss or a repression that is relative to all that refers to the social relations of production. These critiques direct themselves to his notion of hegemonic logic because, in them, the ultimate determination of the capitalist mode of production would tend to be erased. However, I consider that Laclau does not simply promote a story that, by itself, would be capable of conveying a popular and transformative project. On the contrary, and taking into account the problem of fantasy and ideology previously discussed, I suggest that the political project cannot be totally separated from the social relations of production and of its mode of reproduction. In this sense, my reading of Laclau's proposal would have to be intervened by the logic that I extract from Lacan's teachings which can be summarized as:

a) There is no necessary relation between the social relations of production and the possible subjects of emancipation.
b) This is no impossible relation between social relations of production and the possible subjects of emancipation.
c) There is a contingent relationship between the social relation of production and the possible subjects of emancipation.

Therefore, a transformative project could only occur when subjects produce (in a contingent manner – not necessary or impossible) a relationship with truth that is transplanted into the social relations of production. This does not mean reducing the relationship to mere contingency since the objective interests are, indeed, present in this proposal without affects with the order of necessity. The challenge consists in "inventing" a new link between the possible subjects of emancipation and the order of domination. I say inventing, in the strongest sense of the word, since previous historical models (although they can be key references) cannot be reproduced. I suggest that we must attend to the social relations of production when thinking of emancipatory projects. We could even complicate the matter further since capitalist discourse, by definition, does not have a quilting point (*point de capiton*). It is as if there were a permanent metonymy that is displaced. That is precisely where its limited condition resides, by promising to satisfy the lack with some object that immediately relaunches dissatisfaction – this does not have a *point de capiton*. As a consequence, leftist and national-popular movements must ask themselves this question: how should we proceed if politics always demands an anchoring point? On the one hand, and as Lacan himself pointed out, we are dominated by a discourse that does not have an anchoring point and reproduces itself without limit. In other words, it does not have an exterior nor a historical beyond.

In that sense, with respect to psychoanalysts who argue that psychoanalysis is solely a one-on-one, case-by-case endeavor and that the universal is not a matter that concerns them, I must say that I disagree. I say this because in our present time of the "for all," a new type of social tie is constantly being introduced, which has either *objet a*, *jouissance*, or the death drive as foundational elements. On this point, I think Freud is correct to say in *Civilization and Its Discontents* that Thanatos can defeat Eros. Put in Lacanian terms, capitalist discourse marches towards its decline. It is no longer about the world being unjust but, rather, that it is unsustainable given that it unleashes something that expands uncontrollably in every direction through an absolutely acephalous structure. Moreover, and as I have said before, political discourse (which does need a symbolic anchor) has limited resources with which to intervene. Nevertheless, in order not to fall into indifference, we must not let our guard down or wash our hands of political discourse. On the contrary, we must insist again and again. The challenge is in trying to construct a "non-totalizing all," a *not-all*, as Lacan indicates in his construction of feminine logic – a not-all that would take the form of a heterogeneous will and would combine many singularities.

If psychoanalysts want to continue with the one-on-one, they should take into account these transformations because neoliberalism and its powerful "self-help" discourse is directed to the subject: "This is made for you, you are going to have a unique experience, and you are unmistakable." Lacan already said that "we are all proletariats," referring to the fact that none of us could have a discourse that would link us to the social field. We are proletariats not necessarily because we may work in factories but also because we are separated from the collective since we do not have a discourse that would make possible a social tie. This is the challenge.

What has happened to the left? For decades, the left has felt the weight of its own impotence, simply remaining at the point of reflection and without being able to get rid of a historical path that always returns to the same point. It is also notable that, in response to the effects of globalization, "right-wing Marxists" want to reestablish honor, the family, identities, love for the earth, customs, and more. There is something reactionary in this. One can maintain a certain defense of the family, but I do not understand why there cannot be a trans or homosexual family, for example. I do not believe that the family must be heteronormative; its historical time has concluded. In my view, I find the existence of the family to be convenient for raising children, and on this matter, it seems to me to be a positive invention – a place where one can read the same story to a child and where the child can recognize their differences with adults. On this point, my proposal for a left Lacanianism may be, in a certain sense, conservative because it is open to discussing what deserves to be conserved so that capitalism and neoliberal power do not do away with everything. But my proposal does not aim to be restorative or nostalgic. And as has already been mentioned, when Althusser refers to the ideological state apparatuses, he highlights that the school/family pair had replaced the church. We can now affirm that that pair can no longer be sustained since it seems that the school and the family do not have sufficient consistency to be able to be named as ideological apparatuses given the symbolic decline of authorities. If they do have this sufficient consistency, it has certainly been perforated by the incessant and repetitive flow of social networks.

I insist again that ideology does not occur in a compact way, rather, it maintains a border relationship with fantasy. This consideration is very important when it comes to thinking about the problem of praxis given the slow disintegration that we are witnessing in the field of the social and, therefore, the increasingly difficult possibility that politics intervene in this field, since, in my view, the social and the political do not occur together in a spontaneous way. Even so, I still bring up the challenge in terms of an emancipatory act, basing this on Lacan's analytic discourse. In this way, the notion of the act is key for being able to understand what a transformation would consist of. The act can be defined as a sort of extraordinary forceful entry by the subject which would lead them to the site of the truth as a cause of desire. This act would consist of a subversive operation, according to which the knowing would not be considered a true metalanguage but would, rather, consist of the subject displacing precisely the site of the truth. Understood this way, the act does not refer to an exceptional event, and neither to a miracle or any sort of trauma. The subject suffers from truth even though they might not know it since it has been sedimenting throughout their life through the work of the unconscious. Because of that, the act does not necessarily imply a great disruptive and overwhelming action; it could be the result of a silent and microscopic work that is unexpectedly precipitated. But we can only account for the journey and the consequences of this act retroactively. The materialist theoretical wager that I have attempted to develop would imply a moment of shock to the structure and would not be a praxis that was the result of any dialectical mediation. Rather, this act would suppose bearing in mind the relationship between fantasy (primary condition) and ideology (secondary elaboration), given both that neither instance totally superimposes itself and that they are not totally separate operations.

In any case, we should remember, with Hegel, that the owl of Minerva flies at night and that perhaps, sooner or later, the worldwide fracture of inequality will be introduced into the "all" of the pandemic, and the millions of human beings that have no possible inscription might eventually be able to become agents of a new social antagonism. I do not rule out that, after a period of fear and confusion has passed, new rebellions may begin in spite of not being certain whether or not they will have a political organization that would orient them. Everything will depend on the new political inventions and on the reappropriations that can be made with respect to previous egalitarian moments, in the continuous and discontinuous temporality marked, in Lacanian terms, by the expression to which I always refer: *what I will have been for what I am in the process of becoming*. This temporality should concern both the radical singularity of each subject and the transformative project of the common, expressed in the two knots that I have shown between community-society-state and mourning-memory-desire.

In relation to all of this, no doubt, the term emancipation is highly problematic due to the questions that it provokes and also because it alludes to the inaugural traces present in Kant, which are indicative of a tradition that carries on even to Marx. To these traces, I add Freud and Lacan's "bad news." Can emancipation exist without transcendental law and without teleology? And if it cannot, in what sense would it take place? As I have argued in various texts, there is no historical necessity that would determine emancipation and impose itself as a horizon; similarly, there is no fixed path that would lead to that goal. Indeed, not even does the history of the human species itself allow for establishing any hope regarding emancipation coming to pass beyond phantasmatic mirages that have a certain utopian tinge. The keys to history present all the arguments for never expecting it. But having said this, a political ethic that should be indelible in any militant action would always be the bearer of a wager without guarantee in favor of the historical realization of equality and justice. Even though equality and justice are often presented with negative examples that highlight what is unequal or unjust, precisely the inapprehensible character of both categories should serve as an impulse for desire in relation to the fulfillment of these postulates. Paraphrasing Kant, beyond the irreducible differences between his philosophy of history and that conceptualized by Marx, Freud, and Lacan, we should not give up on the desire for equality and justice, even if we may not have a positive definition of them. In the desire/duty equation, both a danger and that which could save us is at stake.

So, emancipation?

Yes, because you can and should. At the end of the day, not desiring the always interminable time of emancipation would be like not desiring at all.

Chapter 14

Note

"Discourse" is a term that, in a general sense, designates the form in which deter-mined and effective statements are produced, as well as their consequences. We speak of medical discourse, political discourse, scientific discourse, etc., but we should be clear that Lacan speaks of discourse in a more fundamental way. In the first place, discourse without words – that is, a frame or structure that implies places or terms and that is the matrix of any act in which a word is taken. The signifier is the cause of the discourse since it is in the capture that the signifier exerts on speaking beings where the minimal operations that make discourse pos-sible are established. Discourse, as a social bond, supports itself in language. If the unconscious is structured like a language, discourse is the fundamental frame that makes it possible for each individual to find the necessary barrier to *jouissance,* to constitute the capitalism bond. Perfect crime or social emancipation. Discourse is how each of us inhabits language. No social tie exists outside of discourse because the subject and the other do not have any medium that would establish their bond in language.

If psychosis is outside of discourse and not of language, this is because it indi-cates a specific mode of relationship between the subject and the other. In psycho-sis, the subject and the place of the other (if they even meet in language) also find each other outside of the pacts and barriers that introduce the function of discourse. From this perspective, another case of a particular relationship between a subject and other in language and outside of discourse is constituted by a certain type of writing that does not establish a discourse nor a social tie, but that does constitute an attempt at establishing a symbolic barrier to *jouissance.*

In the structure that Lacan presents of the four discourses, the following names appear: hysteric, university, master, and analyst. These discourses rotate non-permutatively (the function like a Klein group, coming and going like clock hands). It follows that, on the one hand, they are radically different from one another, and, on the other hand, none in particular can assume the elimination of the others. It would be possible, in spite of the differences between the four discourses, to think there is a fundamental intelligence between them that would come from their nec-essary character to the structure of the unconscious. Four ways of making social ties in which the unconscious is at play. But this is this way from an exclusively

DOI: 10.4324/9781003409410-15

structural point of view because we cannot ignore the fact that, on the other hand, these discourses have modes of historical emergence, with all that this entails as a crossroads and as conflict. Even though he only presented the structure of capitalist discourse on one occasion, during the final years of his teaching Lacan nevertheless insisted not only on polishing its characterization but, rather, on situating psychoanalysis with respect to it.

On May 12th, 1972, at a conference in Milan titled "On Psychoanalytic Discourse," Lacan made public what he meant by the structure of capitalist discourse. He had been invited by the Institute of Psychology in the School of Medicine and the French Cultural Center, an initiative coordinated by the Italian psychoanalyst Giacomo Contri. From the relationship between the master discourse and its opposite – the analyst's discourse – Lacan showed how, by producing in the master discourse "a little inversion between the S1 and the $, $," capitalist discourse emerges. The following year, in "On the Experience of the Pass," he characterized capitalist discourse as a "certain variety of the master discourse" which is distinguished only "by a very small change in the order of the letters." We note that in both cases he refers to the passage from one discourse to another in terms of a "little inversion" and "small change." The formal smallness that Lacan points to – that inversion between S1 and the $ – gives rise, in reality, to a profound alteration in the meaning of the vectors and in the general functioning of the formula. It is about the rejection of the truth of the discourse since it has inverted the meaning of the vector that connects the site of the truth with the site of the semblance. The agent of the discourse (the site of the semblance) repudiates the determination that it receives from the truth in order to go on to direct it. The semblance is no longer the master signifier that receives its determination of the truth. Rather, it is the subject, enthroned as an agent, that operates over the master signifier placed in the site of the truth. This manipulation of the truth is a rejection of the castration of discourse conducive to establishing a circularity. Due to this continuity, discourse comes to function in a circularity without interruptions. For this reason, and because of the fact that the circuit finds itself oriented towards the left, we can speak of an "uncanny circle." In the master discourse, the master is the signifier and not the subject. On the contrary, in capitalist discourse, thanks to this small deviation, it becomes installed in the position of the agent of the discourse of the subject – the subject-master – giving rise to a perverse form of discourse.

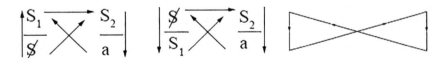

Figure 14.1 – three discourses

1) Master discourse, 2) capitalist discourse, 3) circular movement of capitalist discourse

Index

Page locators in *italics* indicate a figure